CW00428797

the

Icon

Cover: St. Andrei Rublev, Iconographer

By the Same Author

Le lieu du couer, Initiation à la spiritualité de l'Eglise orthodoxe
Les editions du Cerf, Paris, 1989.

Les crétiens et les images
Montéal, Québec, Éditions Paulines, 1992

Etudes iconographiques
Nethen, Belgium, Éditions Axios, 1993

The Image of God the Father in Orthodox Theology and Iconography and
Other Studies
Oakwood Publications, Torrance, California 1995

Heroes
of
the
Icon

Fr. Steven Bigham

Ωakwood ΓPublications

Torrance, California

1998

**Distributed to the trade by: Source Books
ISBN: 1-879038-91-9**

CONTENTS

PREFACE

This is a book that needs to be read by both Orthodox Christians and non-Orthodox alike. This is especially true because of the wide interest in Christian Iconography both among members of the Orthodox Christian Church and those who are not Orthodox Christians. But perhaps the group that will find this book most useful of all will be the increasingly large number of converts to the Orthodox Church. Many things are being written about icons and iconography right now and some of them are of questionable value and validity. Fr. Steven Bigham has produced a book that is grounded solidly in Orthodox Christian theology, and represents the best in Orthodox tradition.

The approach of this book is unique with a view of iconography that is largely not available in other publications. It provides a background in the basics of iconographic study for those unfamiliar with the history and tradition of Orthodox Christian iconography, but it also gives a new perspective to those who already have had some experience and have developed some knowledge of the field. In large part recent books on icons have been concerned with superficial aesthetics, that is they have focused almost entirely on simply describing icons in regard to their visual characteristics. Sometimes these descriptions have included brief discussion of the historical and cultural setting of the particular icons under study but the theological and spiritual dimension of the icons have been largely ignored. The few books that have been written purporting to describe the spirituality of icons and their use, have been superficial and trite. In some cases things have been written by non-Orthodox authors that have bordered on or even crossed over into heretical views and practices.

In his first two chapters Fr. Bigham establishes a solid basis for a theology of the icon. This then serves as a foundation for the bulk of the work which is concerned with icons as the spiritual products of holy lives. This book gives a unique introduction to the world of the iconographers themselves. The painters of icons come alive as one sees their heroism, and in some cases their suffering. The link between the icons themselves and the community that produced them is clearly established. One sees that icons are not just single works of art existing in isolation. For the first time the general public can get a sense that the painters who have produced the icons are not only real people but truly heroic people. In some cases, as for example the martyrs of the iconoclastic period, their heroism is truly humbling. The lives of the heroic iconographers presented in this work helps to dispel a common misunderstanding that iconography is, at best, a sentimental and nostalgic form of art, somewhat quaint and rather romantic, and, at worst, a folk craft only slightly more sophisticated than the paint-by-numbers kits sold in some of the hobby stores. In the lives of the heroes of iconography we see the deep and profound spiritual basis to their work. We come to realize that the painting of icons is not a hobby nor a commercial enterprise. It is a vocation, — both a gift and a calling from God. As such it is a sacramental activity. It is important, however to recognize that Orthodox Iconographers never function as individual artists but instead are first and foremost members of the community of faith, the Holy Orthodox Church.

There are many reasons why anyone who is interested in Orthodox iconography should read this book.. Those who hopefully aspire to paint icons themselves will be moved by this book to look into their own lives and examine their motives in light of the high calling that a true iconographer must live. Those who see orthodox iconography as a quaint folk art, those who see Orthodox Iconography as a nice way of decorating a house of worship should learn from this book the true depth of iconographic spirituality.

Fr. Lester Michael Bundy
Professor Religious Studies
Regis University
Director of the St. John Chrysostom
Institute of Orthodox Studies

INTRODUCTION

This work has been conceived as a three-stone jeweled ring: in the middle is a large diamond, and on either side are two smaller sapphires. 1) The diamond is the chapter "The Heroes of the Icon," which also gives its name to the book as a whole. At various times, I have seen references to an ancient Russian document about holy iconographers, but I have never been able to find it. And, of course, behind every icon stands an iconographer whose presence, though somewhat obscured by the light shining from the icon, is often forgotten. I therefore decided to undertake an independent study of saint iconographers, hoping to find along the way that elusive Russian document. The fruit of my research is presented in the following pages, and, yes, I did find the Russian document. Not only one, but two of them. They are also presented in the annex. Unfortunately, the original document on which they are based has been lost.

As I progressed in my research, it was obvious that there were many other people who, though not painters, clustered around the holy iconographers and who supported them by their theological defenses of the icon against detractors or by their blood as martyrs and confessors. It seemed, therefore, only natural to include them as well. Other well-known people are also associated with the icon throughout history but are not considered saints; I called them masters of the icon. Finally, my research turned up an interesting category of painters whose names, by an accident of history, have been preserved but who are otherwise nearly unknown .

All of these glowing faces stand behind the icon: some shine more brilliantly than others; the most radiant of whom, however, is Saint Andrei Rublev (and why not his friend, Daniel Chorny?). They are in fact the real icons. Not being a painter, I cannot take up myself the challenge I would like to lay down to Orthodox iconographers: why not paint a "cast-of-thousands" icon, having the same dimensions as Saint Andrei's Trinity icon, which would show all the heroes of the icon gathered around an image of the Holy Face? Let anyone who hears the call of the Lord take up paint and brush!

2) One of the sapphires is "The Three Dogmatic Mo-

ments of the Icon." Iconography is an eminently theological art. As such, it sets side-by-side both the legal prohibition of images of God or of any creature—the second commandment—and the Christian production images—icons of Jesus the Son of God and of his friends. It seemed a good idea, therefore, to delve into the historical and doctrinal foundation that not only permits but requires what at first seems to be a contradiction. The result of that reflection is found in this article. It is often the case that the content of an article is not new, but rather brings together scattered elements into a coherent whole. I hope that this article falls into that category. Anyone who has studied the history of iconography knows about, or has heard of, the content of "The Three Moments..." I cannot, however, remember a text which links the history and theology of the three events mentioned here so as to form a solid foundation for any thinking on the subject.

3) The third stone, the second sapphire, of the ring is the lexicon. Many words are casually used to describe icons. Sometimes people know what they mean, and sometimes not; sometimes people use words to sound knowledgeable, just for effect. There is nonetheless a lot of confusion so I thought it would be useful to attempt to define some of the more common terms as they apply to icons. That mini-dictionary is "Iconography: a Lexicon." I must say that the discussion of each adjective is the result of my own reflection; therefore, it is personal. On the other hand, it is not my goal simply to present my opinion. Although I have personal opinions and tastes, I can distinguish them from what I think is Holy Tradition. It is my intention to discuss these words in the context of twenty centuries of reflection on, and artistic production of, Christian art. Taking my stand squarely in the midst of that long tradition, I hope, at least, to have been a faithful spokesman of the mind of the Church.

I therefore submit this work to you the reader and to the Church for your evaluation and edification.

A special thanks to Thomas Drain whose translation skills were of great help in getting Russian texts into English.

Chapter 1

The Three Dogmatic Moments of the Icon

I. Introduction

The existence of the icon, especially the icon of Christ the Son of God, poses a fundamental question to the Christian Tradition: How is it possible to make an image of God? By confessing that Jesus of Nazareth is "the image of the invisible God" (Col. 1:15), fully God and fully man, the Biblical and ecclesial Tradition identifies an image of Christ with an image of God. More exactly, an image of Christ is an image of the image of God. The images of the saints or events, whether from the Bible or Church history, are in a different category because they represent only human beings. Therefore, the Church has had to define its thinking about the existence of these two categories of Christian images: those of saintly men and women and those of the God-Man.

At the time of the iconoclastic crisis of the 8th and 9th centuries, the Church was forced to formulate its theology about the contested practice of making and venerating images. But well before this time, the Church had already been producing images of Christ, the saints, and events from sacred history, without, however, giving much serious, theological reflection to this activity. Nonetheless, during the bloody struggle between the iconoclasts—those who denied the possibility of making Christian images and venerating them, on the one hand—and the iconodules—those who affirmed this possibility, on the other—the Church in the Latin West and in the Greek East defined the meaning of its artistic activity in human thoughts and words. The Byzantine iconoclasts attacked icons, first those of Christ and then of any saint, by identifying them with idols. By the voices of John of Damascus, the Second Council of Nicaea, Theodore the Studite, and Nicephorus of Constantinople, the iconodules answered the attack by affirming not only the possibility but the necessity of making the image of God-made-flesh as well as images of his friends, the saints. To refuse such an iconographic tradition was equated to attacking the heart of the Gospel itself, that is, the Incarnation.

We live, even today, in and by that Tradition, contested but strengthened and affirmed during the iconoclastic period. In order to understand that Tradition theologically, however, we must clearly understand the meaning of the three dogmatic moments that underlie it: 1) Mount Sinai, around 1270 B. C.[1], the prohibition of any image of the invisible God; 2) Nazareth, about 4 B. C.[2], the passage from the invisibility of God to his visibility; and 3) Nicaea, 787 A. D.[3], the definition of the nature of the icon and its veneration. Those who live in and by the ecclesial Tradition about icons believe that God acted in these historical moments to express his will. The revelations that resulted from these divine interventions form, among other things, the dogmatic foundation of the icon. We will now examine these three moments so as to understand better the nature of the icon, that image which carries mystery within it.

II. The First Dogmatic Moment

The first dogmatic moment took place on Mount Sinai around 1270 B. C. when the invisible God prohibited the production of any kind of image of himself.

A. The invisible God

At the moment when a group of ragtag refugees was transformed into the People of God, the Lord made himself known to Moses and to Israel as the invisible God, invisible in his very nature, having no form whatsoever and not representable by anything in creation. It is important to note that this revelation, the second commandment, took the verbal form of a negation. God is not visible; he has no form whatsoever. We have here the cornerstone of negative or apophatic theology, which clearly prefers to speak of God by saying what he is not—invisible—rather than what he is. We do not know, and cannot know, what God is in his essence, his being, that is, in positive terms. We know something about his action in creation, but his nature is impenetrable. In Ps. 17:11[4], we read that "he made darkness his covering around him, his canopy thick clouds dark with water"; Ps. 96:2 says that "clouds and thick darkness are round about him... ."

It is possible to speak about God in positive terms, but in that case, the words we attribute to God have a symbolic, non-literal meaning: Ps. 22:1, "The Lord is my shepherd..."; 2 Sam. 22:31-33, "... he is a shield for all those who take refuge in him ... and who is a rock, except our God... this God is my strong refuge... ." With imagery, it is possible to evoke God's presence through indirect signs: the ark of the covenant, a throne, even a hand. These are not really images of God but rather verbal and pictorial indicators that make us think of him who is invisibly present. However, no direct image of him, no word, can capture God and express him.

The revelation of God's invisibility is contained in the second commandment and takes various forms in the first books of the Bible.

1. Exod. 20:4-5, "You shall not make yourself a graven image or any likeness of anything that is in heaven above, or that is in the earth beneath, or that is in the water under the earth; you shall not bow down to them or serve them; for I the Lord your God am a jealous God. . . "

2. Exod. 34:17, "You shall make for yourself no molten gods."

3. Lev. 19:4, "Do not turn to idols or make for yourselves molten gods: I am the Lord your God."

4. Lev. 26:1, "You shall make for yourselves no idols and erect no graven image or pillar, and you shall not set up a figured stone in your land to bow down to them; for I am the Lord your God."

5. Deut. 4:15-18, "Therefore take good heed to yourselves. Since you saw no form on the day that the Lord spoke to you at Horeb out of the midst of the fire, beware lest you act corruptly by making a graven image for yourselves, in the form of any figure, the likeness of male or female, the likeness of any beast that is on the earth, the likeness of any winged bird that flies in the air, the likeness of anything that creeps on the ground, the likeness of any fish that is in the water under the earth."

B. Two sorts of idols

In a world where all divinities made themselves visible in material images, sculpted or painted, the Lord of Israel proclaimed that he was utterly other than the gods of the nations—those false gods, those "godlets," those nothings—and that he was radically unlike them. By seeking to differentiate himself from the false gods of the nations, the Lord blocked the road that led to the human mistake of attempting to create his image, in which— mistakenly—they might try to "see" him (or think that they saw him). He forbade his people even to try to produce his image. God did not so much prohibit the making of his image—such a thing was completely impossible anyway: Isa. 40:18, "To whom then will you liken God, or what likeness compare with him?" He forbade rather the trying to do such a thing. To attempt to assimilate the Lord of Israel to something created would already be a blasphemy, and the resulting material image of such an artistic activity would be an idol. We therefore have the first definition of an idol: a material image of the God of Israel.

There is, on the other hand, a second sort of idol: a material image of a being who dares take the place—unique and jealously guarded—of the God of Israel. It is absolutely forbidden for Israel to recognize these false, rival gods and their images or to give them any kind of worship since they have the effrontery of contesting the throne of the Lord God. The only God, the Creator, he who called Abraham and established the covenant with Moses and Israel, requires total devotion from his people. The images of pagan divinities proclaim two insulting and insufferable falsehoods right in God's face: 1) other gods exist beside the God of Abraham, Isaac, and Jacob and 2) material images can make him visible, can capture him, and show him forth in some created thing. The people of God must forever reject idolatrous, material images.

C. An idolatrous attitude

The second commandment forbids not only the making of idolatrous images but also the worship given to them. God, and he alone, can receive worship, that is, *latreia*. Any created thing that is worshipped, whether an image or not—the sun for example—automatically becomes an idol, and those who worship it attract God's anger. The Biblical texts speak of service offered to these gods, of bowing down before them, as an expression of misdirected worship. Other corporal gestures can also be idolatrous. Two things are therefore necessary for anyone to be guilty of idolatry, the supreme sin against God: 1) an image that is claimed to be of God or of a pagan deity, or to be the pagan deity itself, and 2) worship—whether overtly expressed or not—of that false image.

No one would break God's law by simply being in

the presence of an idol—remember St. Paul in Athens—handling various objects, or gesturing to persons—see Gen. 49:8 where Jacob blesses his sons and says, "Judah, your brothers shall praise you...your father's sons shall bow down before you." The essential goal of the second commandment is this: to protect the worship of the invisible God by forbidding an idolatrous, psychological attitude expressed in words or bodily gestures toward a material image of God or a pagan divinity.

Even though the revelation of the God of Israel as essentially invisible and the prohibition of idolatrous images are right from the beginning the foundation of the Biblical experience of God, the people of Israel took a certain time and had to go through several testings before they learned to flee gods made with human hands and to rely only on him who revealed himself at Mount Sinai. It seems that Israel did faithfully obey the first part of the injunction by not making an image of God himself. The Israelites never tried to do the impossible: force God to traverse the gulf between the visible and the invisible and capture him in a material image. The Bible at least does not speak of such a violation, and archaeologists have never found an image suspected of being of the God of Israel.

D. The desire to see God

We understand better now the scope and content of the first dogmatic moment, Mount Sinai, on which the icon stands: God is essentially invisible, his material image is nonexistent, and every effort to make such an image is absolutely forbidden. Nonetheless, despite the Biblical intransigence toward images of God or of gods made with human hands, we can clearly see in the Old Testament a tension between the refusal to visualize God and a great desire, to see him.

We read about certain Biblical events, called

theophanies, in which, apparently, God manifests himself to his servants in a more or less visible form. These theophanies can be divided into four categories: apparitions 1) of the angel of the Lord, 2) of God to someone "face to face," 3) of the divine energies, and 4) in human form.

1. Apparitions of the angel of the Lord

According to certain passages, God in the form of an angel, often called "the angel of the Lord," showed himself and spoke to someone. The best known of these episodes is no doubt the theophany of the three mysterious visitors who came to see Abraham and announced that Sara would have a son (Gen. 18-19:29). In the Biblical story, there is a real ambiguity about the identity of these visitors. Sometimes, the author calls them "the angels," sometimes, "the men," sometimes all three "the Lord." Sometimes he distinguishes between them by designating one "the Lord" and the two others by another name. Even though the Bible says clearly that "the Lord appeared to Abraham," the author is obviously ill at ease having to describe an event in which God is seen physically. By adopting these diverse designations for the visitors, the author preserves the mystery of God's presence and invisibility and soothes his own anxiety.

Other passages alternate between "the Lord" and "the angel of the Lord":

1) Gen. 22:1-19 The two designations indicate that God spoke to Abraham but did not appear to him. The one and the other, "the Lord" and "the angel of the Lord," order Abraham to sacrifice Isaac and then not to sacrifice him.

2) Gen. 16:7-16 The Lord/the angel of the Lord met Hagar in the desert and announced that she would have a son Ishmael.

3) Judg. 6:11-24 The angel of the Lord/the Lord appeared to Gideon and convinced him to save Israel.

4) Judg. 13:1-22 The Lord/the angel of the Lord/the man of God/the man announced the birth of Samson to Manoah and his wife.

2. "Face-to-face" apparitions

The Biblical expression "face-to-face" is ambiguous: it can have a concrete or figurative meaning. It can mean simply "intimate" without any concrete connotation of directly seeing someone or something. Deut. 34:10 has this metaphorical meaning: "And there has not arisen a prophet since in Israel like Moses whom the Lord knew face to face... ." We will set aside such passages and study only those that have a more concrete sense, implying a vision in which something/someone is seen.

Gen. 32:23-31 "... and a man wrestled with him until the breaking of the day .... So Jacob called the name of the place Peniel, saying, 'For I have seen God face to face and yet my life is preserved.'" Who was this someone: a real man, God himself, or an angel—as we read in Hos. 12:5? According to the Genesis text, this person, refused to give his name when Jacob asked for it, thus leaving the mystery of his identity hanging in the air. In this episode, Jacob senses the presence of God, but we hesitate to go so far as to say that this was God in the form of a man. By identifying the unknown wrestler with an angel, the subsequent Biblical tradition, as recorded in Hos. 12:5, resolves the problem and thus preserves the mystery of God.

Num. 12:6-8 "And he said, 'Hear my words: If there is a prophet among you, I the Lord make myself known to him in a vision, I speak with him in a dream. Not as with my servant Moses; he is entrusted with all my house. With him I speak mouth to mouth, clearly, and not in dark speech; and he beholds the form of the Lord.'" Here God spoke to Moses and showed himself to him. The conversation "mouth to mouth" contrasts with "dark speech." The expression can carry a figurative sense also; the last line says that Moses saw the Lord's form, and that

Israel was not able to see when God appeared at Horeb (Deut. 4:18). Even though the Hebrew says "form of the Lord," the Septuagint and the Syriac translations speak of the "glory" of God, thus lessening the rather jolting anthropomorphism.

3. Apparitions of the divine energies

In a series of theophanies, the Lord showed himself in a brilliance, in a light, a glory, sometimes accompanied with a voice but without any human form. The Orthodox Christian tradition calls this luminosity the "divine energies." These visions conform perfectly to the theological distinction of St. Gregory Palamas, bishop of Thessalonica in the 14th century in Byzantium, between the unknown and unknowable essence of God and his manifestations in creation through his energies.

Exod. 3:2-6 God/the angel of God met Moses in the burning bush and spoke to him from the fire, but Moses only saw fire.

Exod. 19:9-25 The Lord met the people of Israel on Mount Sinai and spoke through a thick cloud. Lightening, a cloud of smoke and fire covered the mountain from which the Lord spoke. Exod. 23:16-18 adds that the glory of the Lord, like a devouring fire, veiled the mountain during seven days.

Several passages from Ezekiel mention the visions of the prophet in which he saw the glory of the Lord. Ezek. 10:1-5 tells of the prophet's vision about the restoration of the Temple which had been destroyed by Nebuchadnezzar: "... and the house [the Temple] was filled with the cloud, and the glory of the Lord."

4. Apparitions in human form

In this last category, we have very descriptive theophanies. They are visions where the prophet sees not only the glory of God but also a human form. The following question thus comes to the fore: If God is invisible and if no image of him is possible because no created thing resembles him, how is it that the prophets had anthropomorphic visions? We will come back to this question after having studied the following texts.

Four passages state that several prophets "saw the Lord" without, however, saying that a human form was visible. These texts, though, are similar to others in which a prophet claims to have seen a human form.

Isa. 6:1-5, "In the year that King Uzziah died, I saw the Lord sitting upon a throne, high and lifted up; and his train filled the temple."

1 Kings 22:19, "Micaiah said [to the king of Israel], 'Therefore hear the word of the Lord: I saw the Lord sitting on his throne, and all the host of heaven standing beside him on his right hand and on his left.'"

Amos 9:1, "I saw the Lord standing beside the altar, and he said … ."

Exod. 24:9-11, "Then Moses and Aaron, Nadab, and Abihu, and seventy of the elders of Israel went up, and they saw the God of Israel; and there was under his feet as it were a pavement of sapphire stone … ."

The prophet Ezekiel goes farther than the others (Ezek. 1:26-28). In Ezekiel's first vision, we hear, "And above the firmament over their heads [the four living beings], there was the likeness of a throne, in appearance like sapphire; and seated above the likeness of a throne was a likeness as it were of a human form. And upward from what had the appearance of his loins I saw as it were gleaming bronze, like the appearance of fire enclosed round about; and downward from what had the appearance of his loins I saw, as it were, the appearance of fire, and there was brightness round about him. Such was the appearance of the likeness of the glory of the Lord."

Ezekiel had a second vision similar to the first one, Ezek. 8:1-5, in which he mentions again "the appearance of a man." This latter expression is a translation of the

Greek, whereas the Hebrew says "the appearance of fire." In different passages, when describing his other visions or when referring to the first one, Ezekiel speaks only of having seen the glory of the Lord. The prophet himself and the Biblical tradition are still ill at ease when dealing with this phenomenon.

The vision of the prophet Daniel goes the farthest in giving God a human form, Dan. 7:9-14.

> As I looked, thrones were placed and one that was ancient of days took his seat; his raiment was white as snow, and the hair of his head like pure wool; his throne was fiery flames, its wheels were burning fire. A stream of fire issued and came forth from before him.... . I saw in the night visions, and behold, with the clouds of heaven there came one like a son of man, and he came to the Ancient of Days and was presented before him. And to him was given dominion and glory and kingdom, that all peoples, nations, and languages should serve him; his dominion is an everlasting dominion, which shall not pass away, and his kingdom one that shall not be destroyed.

Daniel is the most daring of the prophets and does not seem to hesitate to describe God as a man. Nonetheless, he protects himself from the charge of blasphemy and shows his own anxiety by saying that this vision was not direct or seen with his own eyes. It was one of "the visions of my head," "in the night visions." In other words, it was a dream that disturbed and tormented his soul; we might even say a nightmare.

III. The Second Dogmatic Moment

The second dogmatic moment took place at Nazareth in the year 4 B. C. and is the moment of God's voluntary passage from invisibility to visibility.

A. Two canons of interpretation

The following is a fundamental principle of the

Christian understanding of the Bible: the Old Testament is read and interpreted in the light of the New. In other words, the history of Israel is understood as the preparation and announcement of the coming of the Messiah. This principle is relevant to the question that we are studying here: the invisibility and the image of God. We have in the New Testament the most categorical texts stating that no one has ever seen God. It is also in the New Testament that we have the largest number of texts on God's invisibility.

At least ten New Testament passages directly or indirectly support the truth that the Old Testament only obscurely expresses, namely that God is invisible. John 1:18 ("No one has ever seen God; the only Son, who is in the bosom of the Father, he has made him known") sets out two canons for interpreting the Scriptures. First of all, God's invisibility is affirmed in an absolute way. Whatever was the content of the prophetic visions, the prophets did not see God. Consequently, no image of God based on those visions is possible. Secondly, we know the Father through the Son: "... for through him we both have access in one Spirit to the Father" (Eph. 2:18). The Son is the instrument of all the Father's activity, the mediator of all knowledge about him, in the Old Testament as in the New: "all things were made through him, and without him was not anything made that was made" (John 1:3). The ancient Church, around 350, expressed this belief visually in the mausoleum of St. Constantia in Rome where a mosaic shows Christ giving the new Law to Ss. Peter and Paul.[5] In a similar mosaic in the same church, a man that has the same features as those of Christ in the first mosaic is giving the Law to Moses. The intention is obviously to indicate that the two men are the same person: Christ is the author of both Laws.[6] Around the 11th century in France, two wall paintings in a Romanesque church show a man dressed as Christ with a cruciform halo; he is blessing Noah and giving the Law to Moses.[7]

Three other texts bear witness to the truth that no one has ever seen God:

1 Tim. 1:17, "To the King of ages, immortal, invisible, the only God, be honor and glory for ever and ever. Amen."

1 Tim. 6:16, "... the King of kings and the Lords of lords, who alone has immortality and dwells in unapproachable light, whom no man has ever seen or can see."

1 John 4:12, "No man has ever seen God."

B. Toward the visibility of God

We now arrive at the event that constitutes the passage from God's invisibility to his voluntary visibility: Nazareth, the Annunciation when Gabriel announced to Mary that she would be the mother of the Messiah and when she accepted this calling. It is the moment of the Incarnation.

The New Testament treats this event, that is, the beginning of the earthly life of the Son of God, in two ways: 1) in narrative, Matt. 1-2 and Luke 1-2 and 2) through theological explanation, John 1:1-18. These two ways of presenting God's work—the historical event and the theological interpretation—are perfectly in line with the characteristics of Biblical revelation. We see the same pattern at Sinai: God called his people from Egypt and established a covenant with Israel; the rest of the Old Testament is a meditation on the meaning, application, and implications of this founding event. We will see later that the third dogmatic moment of the icon also conforms to this pattern. What concerns us now, however, is the implication of the Incarnation for God's visibility and for the possibility of making an image of him.

Two evangelists, Matthew and Luke, tell the story of the Son of God's first earthly moments, how he assumed human nature, became what he was not before without ceasing to be what he was before. This passage took place in silence, in private, and unknown to most. Mary, no doubt, was not even aware of the full meaning of what Gabriel announced to her. Nonetheless, the central event of human history took place.

The text of John 1:14 presents the theological interpretation: "And the Word became flesh and dwelt among us, full of grace and truth; we have beheld his glory, glory as of the only Son from the Father." The two key terms, *Word* and *beheld,* contain the essence of the second dogmatic event of the icon: the passage to visibility. The Christian doctrine of the Trinitarian God teaches that the Word of God, existing from all eternity in the bosom of the Father, shares totally the divine nature of the Father, one of whose essential characteristics is invisibility. At the moment of the Incarnation, however, the Word took on everything that had to do with human nature, including visibility. John continues in his first letter (1 John 1:1-4) to accentuate the sensory aspects of his experience of the Incarnation:

> That which was from the beginning, which we have heard, which we have seen with our eyes, which we have looked upon and touched with our hands, concerning the word of life—the life was made manifest, and we saw it, and testify to it, and proclaim to you the eternal life which was with the Father and was made manifest to us—that which we have seen and heard we proclaim also to you, so that you may have fellowship with us... .

In Matt. 13:16-17 (see also Luke 10:23-24), Christ explained the privileged position of the apostles in relation to the people of the Old Testament: "But blessed are your eyes, for they see, and your ears, for they hear. Truly, I say to you, many prophets and righteous men longed to see what you see, and did not see it, and to hear what you hear, and did not hear it."

28

The Fathers (from St. Ignatius of Antioch, around 105, to St. John of Damascus, around 730) affirmed the Christian belief about God's becoming visible. In order to resist those who taught false doctrines, Ignatius recommended to Polycarp that he look for

> Christ, the Son of God; who was before time, yet appeared in time; who was invisible by nature, yet visible in the flesh; who was impalpable, and could not be touched, as being without a body, but for our sakes became such, might be touched and handled in the body; who was impassible as God, but became passible for our sakes as man; and who in every kind of way suffered for our sakes.[8]

St. John of Damascus: "It is obvious that when you contemplate God becoming man, then you may depict Him clothed in human form. When the invisible One becomes visible to flesh, you may then draw his likeness."[9] We therefore have in the event of Nazareth the dogmatic basis of doing what was impossible and forbidden before: making an image of God. Note that the initiative for this change came from God himself. It was not a necessity or a human demand but a divine act that is the foundation of the artificial[10] image of God, the icon of Christ.

C. The second commandment modified

Must we understand, as a result, that the second commandment no longer has any force, has been revoked? No, not at all. The event of Nazareth did not abolish the prohibition against making images of God but only added an amendment to it. It is still impossible and forbidden to make an image of God in his divinity. The Father and the Holy Spirit are still invisible and without image; they may be symbolized, but not imaged. The Son, on the other hand, by taking on visible human nature, modified—but did not abolish—the second commandment. As we have seen elsewhere, the Son is the only opening, the only path to the Father, the only one who can make the Father known to men.

The Son, then, is the only one, the only "thing" that gives visibility to the Father.

Concerning the visibility of God, several New Testament passages bear witness to the Son's unique role: John 12:45, "... and he who sees me sees him who sent me"; John 14:8-12, "He who has seen me has seen the Father..."; Col. 1:15, "He is the image of the invisible God." He who was and is invisible, without an artificial image, remains so. He, however, who was invisible, but who became visible in his humanity, remains visible, and we can paint his material image. To deny this statement or to weaken its force has always been seen by the Church as an attack on the reality of the Incarnation itself. It is not difficult therefore to understand why Orthodox Christians during the iconoclastic crisis (726-843), and at all times, have always resisted, even to martyrdom, those who brought into question the holy doctrine and balanced practice of iconography.

D. Two visions of the Book of Revelation

The Book of Revelation seems to maintain the distinction between the invisible Father and Spirit and the visible Christ by the way it describes two theophanies: Rev 1:9-20 and Rev 4. In the first, John sees Christ, "one like a son of man," in human form, and describes him physically. By reproducing the symbolism of the Old Testament and by clothing Christ in the features of the Ancient of Days from Daniel, John seems to want to identify the subject of the Old Testament Theophanies with Christ:

> ... clothed with a long robe and with a golden girdle round his breast; his head and hair were white as white wool, white as snow; his eyes were like a flame of fire, his feet were like burnished bronze, refined as in a furnace, and his voice was like the sound of many waters; in his right hand he held seven stars, from his mouth issued a sharp two-edged sword, and his face was like the sun shining in full strength.

This time in imagery, the New Testament bears witness to the principle already set out, the first canon of interpretation: the obscurities of the Old Testament are to be interpreted in the light of the New.

In the second vision, however, Christ himself introduces John into heaven, in front of a throne. Here John avoids all anthropomorphisms. Does he attribute to God the Father the non-human characteristics of the Old Testament theophanies? The text is not totally clear. On the throne, there is "one who is seated" who "appeared like jasper and carnelian, and round the throne was a rainbow that looked like an emerald." The farthest John goes toward giving a human form to the "one seated on the throne" is seen in the hand, as we often see in ancient Christian and Jewish images: "And I saw in the right hand of him who was seated on the throne a scroll...."

E. Seeing and hearing

Even though the passage from God's invisibility to his visibility in the Incarnation of the Word was accomplished in a second, at the very beginning of the work of salvation, Christians did not immediately understand this event, so it seems, as an occasion permitting them to make an image of the God-made-flesh. At least, no document, no archaeological monument allows us to affirm that they did make such images. We know very well that they proclaimed what they heard, the Word of God; the New Testament and the writings of the first three centuries show this very clearly. We have seen, all the same, that the apostles did see something, rather someone, and they were very aware of the importance of what they saw. The New Testament does not speak about any proclamation of the Gospel in images, if there was such a visible preaching alongside the oral preaching. It is not impossible, though, that the apostolic Christians did make use of images and drawn symbols. Oral traditions[10] speak about them, but the written sources and archaeology are silent.

On the basis of works of art that archaeologists have discovered and from ancient Christian writings, we know, nonetheless, that from around the year 200 at the earliest some Christians did make images illustrating certain New Testament events (for example, Christ's baptism in the Jordan) in which Christ was directly depicted. Other images represent him symbolically as the Good Shepherd. We know very little about the circumstances that led to the production of the first such images. We know, however, that the practice of making images of Christ and the saints from both Testaments began very early.[11] Theological reflection on this practice came later and in the heat of controversy. It was in the middle of this crisis, known to history as Byzantine iconoclasm, that the Church dipped into the Bible and into its own tradition to make a reasoned and reasonable defense of its artistic activity that ultimately produced the icon. This was the third dogmatic moment of the icon.

IV. The Third Dogmatic Moment

The third dogmatic moment took place at the 7th Ecumenical Council at Nicaea (787) which dealt with the nature of the icon and its veneration.

A. Two victories: theological and historical

The third important dogmatic moment in the formation and the understanding of iconography took place in the city of Nicaea, near Constantinople, in 787. This ecumenical council was called to resolve the iconoclastic crisis that had been raging since 726. In 730, after four years of fruitless negotiations with Patriarch Germanos, the Emperor Leo III the Isaurian took action and commanded the destruction of Christ's image which hung on one of the gates of Constantinople. This act was the first public act of hostility towards Christian images. The controversy ended some 117 years later in 843 when another council, once and for all, restored icons in the churches. During this period, in 787, the 7th Ecumenical Council of Nicaea took place. This council, along with the authoritative witness—John of Damascus, Pope Gregory II, Patriarchs Germanus and Nicephorus, and Theodore Studite—became the reference point concerning Christian images. What the First Ecumenical Council of Nicaea (325) and St. Athanasius of Alexandria are for the dogma of the Trinity, Nicaea II and the authoritative writers are for the doctrine and practice of iconography. Everything that is done or said about the icon must take these sources into consideration because during the heat of the controversy, the Church's holy Tradition about images was clearly expressed. The main lines of the theological vision concerning the icon were established during the Byzantine iconoclastic crisis and still remain the lighthouse and anchor of the ecclesial Tradition on this subject.

In the two previous dogmatic moments, Mount Sinai and Nazareth, the immediate initiative came from God. Following this initiative, the faithful had the task of receiving the revelation and putting it into practice, of allowing the implications and consequences to emerge. In the case of the Council of Nicaea II, God acted indirectly through chosen vessels; this, however, in no way diminishes the authority of the conciliar statements. By firmly believing in Christ's promise to protect the Church against the gates of hell and to guide it in the way of truth, Christians have always believed that an authentic, ecumenical council expresses the will of Christ. As the apostolic council of Jerusalem stated, so say Orthodox Christians about an ecumenical council: "For it has seemed good to the Holy Spirit and to us… ." (Acts 15:28)

The Second Council of Nicaea certainly constitutes a theological victory in favor of icons, but the historical victory was not decided for more than another 50 years. Indeed, Nicaea II set out and confirmed the basic principles of iconography, but the council's authority was not immediately accepted by all and everywhere, despite the fact the pope of Rome and the four eastern patriarchs had been represented. As proof, we need only call attention to the Frankish Church's resistance to the reception of Nicaea II, an opposition the Roman bishops had to fight for a long time; it took 100 years before Nicaea II was accepted universally. It was only in 880 that Nicaea II was recognized as the 7th Ecumenical Council. The distinction between a theological and historical victory is seen in a similar process after the Council of Nicaea in 325, which proclaimed that Christ is "consubstantial" (*homoousios*) with the Father, that is, of the same nature. Nonetheless, the definition of 325 was not definitively accepted until 381 at the Second Ecumenical Council of Constantinople.

B. The historical situation

What was the historical situation at the outbreak of the iconoclastic crisis? We do not intend to go into detail here but to note simply the historical facts that touch on the doctrine of the icon. During seven centuries, Christians had adopted, adapted, and developed a tradition of figurative art in several mediums: paintings, mosaics, frescoes, illuminated manuscripts, bas-relief, etc. Even though this art is not commanded by Christ or the apostles in the Gospel, it finds its theological justification, nonetheless, in the New Testament. The Christian artistic tradition has expressed itself in various ways, according to several styles, regions, and periods it has passed through, and it is the art historian who has the task of studying its material manifestation, its changes, and its continuities in time and space. Now, at the beginning of the 8th century, everywhere in the Christian world, figurative art—iconography—had its place. It had been integrated into the celebration of the sacramental mysteries without provoking any widespread protest movement. Here and there, however, we have certain indications of a hesitation, a hostility towards images, but nothing like the iconoclastic movement that was about to shake the Church.

In 717, a new emperor, Leo III the Isaurian, mounted the throne in Constantinople; in 741, his son, Constantine V, succeeded his father and reigned until 775. These two were robust, competent, energetic, and victorious emperors, and they challenged the Church by claiming that icons were idols and that the veneration shown to them constituted idolatrous worship. The emperors wanted to remove all the icons from the churches and destroy them. The patriarch of Constantinople, St. Germanus, driven by his instinctive reaction, resisted Leo, was deposed, and exiled. For 75 years, the Church was torn by the iconoclastic crisis.

The first resistance from the iconodules was grounded in intuition and instinct. The coherent justification of the artistic tradition, the articulation of a theological vision in words and ideas, had to wait for the maturing of ecclesial thinking on the subject. In other words, the Church lived with its figurative art without really thinking about the how or the why of it. The reasoned and reasonable answer took some time to work out. It was in the fire of the controversy that the Church was forced to react to attacks coming from the first citizen of the Christian world, the emperor, supported by a large section of the episcopate within the empire. The result of this "forced meditation" can be read in the text promulgated by Nicaea II and in the authoritative writings of the great defenders of the icon.

C. The main lines of the definition

Let us now look at the main lines of the decisions drawn up by the 7th Ecumenical Council of Nicaea.

1. The first point in the conciliar definition distinguished between an icon and an idol. As we have already seen in the section on the second commandment, an idol is an image claiming to be of God or of a false god, an image by which worshipers misdirect worship due to God alone toward some other object. The iconoclasts affirmed, along with the Orthodox, that Christ is the Son of God incarnate but, not accepting that the Incarnation modified the second commandment in relation to God's visibility, they did not come to the same conclusion about the icon's legitimacy. The iconoclasts accused the Orthodox of making what the second commandment forbade: an idolatrous image of God. The iconodules replied that the image of Christ is not an idol for two reasons: 1) it is obviously not an image of a false god; 2) it is not the image of the invisible God, of him in his divine, invisible nature, but of him who himself became visible by assuming human nature. An icon of Christ is, in fact, an image of God but in line with the principle of "visibilization" established in the Incarnation.

The opposition of the iconoclasts to icons of the Mother of God and the saints did not have the same basis as the opposition to the icons of Christ. An icon of St. Peter or of the Virgin Mary is obviously not an image of God, but it is nonetheless an image of something on earth, and the iconodules venerated such images. For the iconoclasts, this veneration was idolatry according to the second part of the definition of idolatry: worship directed to anything or anyone other than God. Consequently, they tried to destroy the images of Christ and of the saints—since they were idols—and to suppress their veneration as idolatrous worship.

2. In the second place, the council defined the nature

of the icon, that is, it defined what an icon represents as image. By painting Christ's image, the iconodules were accused of painting an image either of just the divine nature or of just the human nature. These attacks were founded on the dogma of the Council of Chalcedon, in 451, which specified that Christ is fully man and fully God. The fullness of both natures is united in the second Person of the Trinity. An icon is therefore not an image of the Son of God in his divine nature—something that is impossible from all points of view—nor in his human nature alone, separated from his divinity. This last accusation implied the rejection of the Chalcedonian dogma: the union of two natures in one Person.

The Fathers of Nicaea II answered that the icon is not an image either of the divine nature, of the human nature, or of the two natures together. It is not an image of a nature at all, but rather of a Person, the Son of God, in the visible aspect of his human nature. An icon is in the end a portrait—a direct image of a person, divine or human, according to the visible features of his human nature. It answers the questions "Who?" or "Of Whom is this an image?" An icon does not answer the questions "What?" or "Of what is this an image?" The word *who* is linked to a person: Christ, Peter, James, John, etc.; the word *what* is linked to a thing: a nature, a car, an element, a star, etc.

3. The iconoclasts were opposed not only to the existence of icons of Christ, the Mother of God and the saints—which they called idols—but also to the fact that Orthodox Christians venerated them. They accused the iconodules of offering *latreia*, worship, to icons through their gestures of piety: candles, kissing, processions, incense, bowing, etc. They did not distinguish between worship (*latreia*) and veneration (*proskynesis*). For the opponents of iconography, not only is the icon, by its very nature, an idol, but also the attitude and behavior of

Christians towards the image are idolatrous because they offer to persons and objects what belongs to God alone. The Fathers answered by clearly distinguishing between worship due to God alone and veneration that the faithful naturally show to persons or objects worthy of special consideration or respect.

The Fathers of the council invoked many examples from the Bible and secular life in which gestures of respect, such as prostrations, bowing, etc. toward persons do not imply an idolatrous attitude. They quoted the classical case of the emperor and his image. No one gave the name of *idolatry* to the respect shown to the emperor's image, including a Christian emperor's image. The iconoclasts themselves venerated the cross, like the Orthodox, without thinking they were idolatrous. The Jews, who could hardly be suspected of being idol worshipers, venerated, and still venerate at certain feasts, the Torah by prostrating themselves before it. The Fathers simply called attention to the distinction between *latreia* and *proskynesis* —between worship and veneration—in everyday life and applied it to the veneration shown to icons.

4. The iconoclasts thought they were restoring and perpetuating the apostolic tradition, such as they understood it, by saying that the first Christians did not have icons and were even opposed to them. In part, the iconoclasts built their argument on the silence of the New Testament with regard to Christian images. They felt justified in eliminating images from the churches because there was no specific New Testament mention of them, in the sense that neither Christ nor the apostles commanded that they be made. The Church admitted that the Scriptures are silent on the question but defended the practice of making and venerating images as a useful tradition, though not specifically commanded by the Gospel. Such a tradition had been adopted by the

Christians as an aid in the proclamation of the Gospel. The Fathers claimed, however, that this tradition had its theological and historical roots in the apostolic age.

Of all the affirmations of Nicaea II on icons, this last one provokes, even today, great skepticism. To claim that the veneration of icons has a historical basis in the 1st century seems to many specialists today as nothing less than ridiculous. Nonetheless, the Fathers of the council had the intuition that the root, not just of the theology of images but also of the practice of making and venerating icons, goes back to the apostles. We must admit that the silence of the New Testament and of the most ancient Christian writings on the matter as well as the lack of archaeological monuments make it very difficult to defend the historicity of this intuition. Nonetheless, we must not understand the silence of the New Testament to mean that the first Christians were aniconic, meaning that they had no figurative art whatsoever. We do not know if the New Testament Christians used images or symbols in the preaching of the Gospel. We know, however, thanks to Tertullian from North Africa, that around 200 A. D., a catholic bishop—a bishop of the main body of Christians, not a schismatic or heretical group—had an image of the Good Shepherd engraved on a chalice, but we do not know at what time, in what region or in what circumstances Christians began to produce images or symbols. There is no scientific evidence to support the claim that the apostles used such images, but nothing, except speculation, stops us from suspecting that some historical reality exists behind the intuition of the Fathers of Nicaea II. Perhaps archaeology and more in-depth studies will shed new light on this problem which is of the highest possible interest.

5. The iconoclasts affirmed that icons did not deserve veneration because they were made of "dead matter," that it was degrading to associate intimately Christ and the

Mother of God—eminently spiritual persons—with matter. They denied, in reality, that matter can be the vehicle of anything spiritual. The old pagan, philosophical distinction between matter-senses-body-evil and non matter-intellect-spirit-good came back with a vengeance. What a terrible denial, coming from those who accepted that God became flesh in matter and that his glory shown through it! Taking its stand on the Incarnation, the Church affirmed that matter was very much capable of expressing a spiritual reality and of being its carrier. Matter was not "dead" but spirit-bearing.

If God could take to himself a human nature—of necessity also a body—why could not wood, paints, and pieces of colored glass constituting an artificial image of God and his friends, the saints, carry the spiritual presence of those who were thus represented? A "yes" to icons is a "yes" to the Incarnation, and a "no" to icons is also a "no" to the reality of the Incarnation. By rejecting the iconoclastic position, the Church proclaimed that matter in general, and icons in particular, can be "mysterophorous": they can carry and communicate the mysteries of God.

6. Finally, the Fathers made the distinction between the image and the person painted in the image, between the type and the prototype. The iconoclasts, on the other hand, according to their idea of an image, believed that a material image and the person represented are identical. They grounded their attack against the Orthodox on this confusion and accused them of believing that the image of Christ and Christ himself are the same reality. For the iconoclasts, the only real image is the Eucharist where the person represented—Christ—and what represents him—bread—are identical. The response to this attack was very clear: the Orthodox distinguished between the type—the image—and the prototype—the person—represented. There is a difference of nature between the Son of God and a painted piece of wood which constitutes his

material image. Even though the one carries the likeness and name of the other, the one is not the other. Pushed to the limit of their logic, the iconoclasts should have claimed that the emperor and his image were one and the same. The Fathers took up the statement of St. Basil to show the ridiculous character of their opponents' position: "The honor given to the image goes to the prototype."

We see that the full reality of the Incarnation is at the heart of the Orthodox response. By taking on human nature, God opened the way to an art that was not only decorative, pedagogical, and aesthetic but also "mysterophorous," that is, capable of reflecting and transmitting the mysteries of God and of putting us in communion with the persons represented in the image.

NOTES

1. This is the generally accepted date archaeologists and Biblical scholars have arrived at for the Exodus of the Jews from Egypt, thus also for their arrival at Mount Sinai and their reception of the Ten Commandments.

2. Taking into account the gospel indications of times and rulers, this is the date scholars have arrived at for the birth of Christ.

3. This is the date of Seventh Ecumenical Council held at Nicaea in 787.

4. The Psalms are according to the Septuagint, and Biblical quotes are taken from *The Revised Standard Version.*

5. André GRABAR, *Christian Iconography: A Study of Its Origins*, Princeton, N. J., Princeton University Press, 1968, ill. 101.

6. André GRABAR, *Early Christian Art*, New York, Odyssey Press, 1968, ill. 207, p. 192.

7. Anne PRACHE, *L'art roman en France*, Paris, Nouvelles Éditions Mame, 1989, p. 39.

8. Ignatius of Antioch, *Letter to Polycarp* III, the longer ver-

sion, *The Ante-Nicene Fathers* I, Grand Rapids, Michigan, Wm. B. Eerdmans Publishing Co., 1979, p. 94.

9. John of Damascus, *On the Divine Images* I:8, D. Anderson, tr., Crestwood, New York, St. Vladimir's Seminary Press, 1980, p. 18.

10. Note the terminology: The Word of God is from all eternity the *natural* image of the Father. He has the same nature as the Father but is a distinct Person. There is no other example of a natural image in our human experience, for even the relation of human father to human son is one in which the common human nature is broken, fragmented, such that not only are the two persons distinct but they are distinct as broken pieces of human nature. We can call them, in fact, individuals. Adam, and all humans beings, are the *created* images of God, differing from their Prototype in nature—a man is not God—but resembling God sufficiently to be able to reflect him in a way that no other creature can do. Christ the incarnate Word—the natural image of God—having taken on humanity—the created image of God—combines the two images in the incarnation. An icon of Christ is an *artificial* image, meaning that it has been created by man. It is an image of the image of God. The natures of the icon—generally wood and paints—is different from the human and divine natures of the God-man, but there is sufficient resemblance between the type and the Prototype—especially the sharing of the same name along with sufficient similarities between the human form on the icon and Christ's earthly body—to justify the word *image.*

10. See S. Bigham, *Les Chrétiens et les images*, "Les traditions du Nouveau Testament," Montréal, Éditions Paulines, 1992.

11. It is even quite possible that the early Christians copied their "big brothers," the Jews and began to produce images because they saw the Jews doing the same thing in the synagogues, on sarcophagi, and perhaps elsewhere.

Chapter 2

ICONOGRAPHY: A Lexicon

The number of persons who can point out an icon continues to increase. Perhaps they do not know how to define its characteristics clearly, but they know that an icon has a somewhat strange look. An icon is not just like other religious images. In this chapter, we would like to discuss certain key words that are usually associated with icons. By examining these words, we hope to furnish the reader with tools that will make it easier to understand and appreciate the sacred images of the Orthodox Church. We will therefore begin each section with the same sentence: "Orthodox iconography is a _____ art." This sentence will serve as a framework for a series of adjectives that describe the art of the icon.

I. Orthodox iconography is a *theological* art.

The word *theology* is used to designate God's intervention, his acts in the world which have the purpose of getting back his creature, Man, and lifting him up into the Kingdom of Heaven. By using human language, both oral and written, we try to describe and understand what, in fact, is completely beyond our understanding. We cannot resist the temptation to speak about God and his work; we therefore automatically fall into the domain of theology, into *God-talk*. By our words and ideas, we do our best to give a form to the "formless," to paint the mystery of our salvation. Consequently, the content of our words and concepts, that is, the image we paint of the mystery of salvation, must be compared to the experience of those who have already lived the mystery before us. This image must conform to the experience as it has

43

already been described in the Bible, in the writings of the Fathers, in the decisions of the Ecumenical Councils, in the hymns of the Church. If our *God-talk* expresses Holy Tradition, even though our version of that Tradition betrays the accent and the concerns of our time, we will be faithful communicators of that Tradition. We will succeed in opening the experience of the mystery of salvation to our contemporaries. If, on the other hand, our verbal or written image of the mystery clashes with that presented in the experience of the faithful of all time, then our expression will provoke an allergic reaction in the body of the Church and will be rejected.

Just as words and concepts can paint a rational image of the mystery of salvation, a painted image can also show the salvation experience. In the same way as words, colors can paint this same mystery in a visual image and both mediums of expression must be faithful to the Church's experience. Iconography is therefore a theological art because it expresses, represents, makes visible in forms and colors the same content that is expressed in written documents. The only difference is the medium of expression. Both written documents and painted images must express the revelation of God to men. We must understand, however, that this revelation is not a system of thought or ideas but rather an experience, that of the Kingdom of God. God wants to communicate to us the experience of the new humanity inaugurated by Christ. It is the experience of the Transfiguration which passes through the Cross but which ends up in the Promised Land of the Kingdom. The revelation can be expressed in intellectual concepts and in painted images, hence the usefulness of theology in words and icons, but the experience itself is never captured by these means.

Iconography is, therefore, theology in colors[1], and as such, we can apply the same criteria used to describe and evaluate theology in words. Is this or that expression faithful to the experience of the Transfiguration, or do the experience and its expression clash? In other words, is the expression "orthodox" or "heterodox": does it show forth a "right belief" or "another belief"? In exactly the same way, we ask the question of "orthodoxy" or "heterodoxy" about the opinions and writings of various authors. Theologians of the image are therefore just as important as theologians of the word. Too often, we limit the word *theologian* to thinkers, to authors, and we forget the analogous role of painters; their responsibility is just as heavy.

Here is an example which shows what we mean by "iconography, a theological art." On December 9, the Or-

Figure 1. — Saints Joachim and Anna

thodox Church celebrates the Conception of the Mother of God; for the Catholic Church, it is December 8. The icon of this feast shows Joachim and Anne, the parents of Mary, in a loving embrace, sometimes in front of a bed (fig. 1). We often see this image, among other miniatures, on the edge of icons of Mary and the Christ-Child; such border icons represent the important events in Mary's life.[2] By its modesty, this icon teaches us that Joachim and Anne conceived Mary in a natural way through sexual union. It is therefore taken, and rightly so, as an image of Christian marriage, of the holiness to which conjugal union can elevate a husband and wife. On the other hand, the icon of Joachim and Anne has served as a model for "icons" of Mary and Joseph, images whose purpose is to draw attention to the importance and value of Christian marriage, a most eminently laudable intention[3] (fig. 2). However, according to the meaning of the icon of Joachim and Anne, it is clear that the image of Joseph and Mary proclaims a message that is heterodox both from the Catholic point of view and from the Orthodox. The explanation on the back of the image is even more daring than the image itself: "Joseph and Mary ... are shown young and beautiful, and their gesture of mutual tenderness translates their love both virginal and conjugal ... " In other words, according to the written and painted theology of this image, Joseph and Mary conceived Jesus naturally by conjugal union. The most ironic thing of all is that a quotation from Pope Paul VI is also written on the back of the image.

We in no way doubt the sincerity, nor the piety, of those who ordered and painted this image, but by misunderstanding the theological character of iconography, they created, with the best intentions in mind but out of great ignorance, a heterodox "icon."

Here is a second example, from the author's personal experience: A Protestant friend who likes to paint decided to paint an image of Mary. He painted it in the Byzantine style, but purposefully left out the three stars, one on her forehead and one on each shoulder. These stars represent Mary's perpetual virginity. Since Protestants do not generally believe in the perpetual virginity of Mary, this image is an expression of Protestant doctrine. Unfortunately, the image is not exactly an icon since it clashes with Orthodox belief—and Catholic belief also—about Mary. It even potentially clashes with traditional Protestant belief which affirms the virginal conception of Christ.

Thirdly, we have come across images produced by an American company which, to say the least, are somewhat

Figure 2 — Saints Joseph and Mary

surprising.[4] Along with quite traditional images—we could even say icons—of Christ, Mary, and the saints, this company produces and distributes others which put the letters ΙΣ ΧΡ (Jesus Christ, in Greek) and a cruciform halo on figures which, from the Orthodox point of view, even from any serious Christian point of view, are little short of shameful. Non Christians are represented, even a Muslim! Is Islam in favor of such iconography? Jonathan and David, plus two male saints, Sergius and Bacchus, are represented as examples of "holy homosexuality." And more. We can hardly accuse those who produce these images of "uninformed good will." They are in fact very astute business people who, to make a profit, are taking advantage of the public's general lack of knowledge about icons and the religious syncretism of our time. From the American business perspective, it is quite "orthodox" to cash in on a good thing, but from the Orthodox, theological perspective, it is blasphemous.

There are other examples of heterodox or doubtful images, but the ones mentioned above are sufficient to underline once again that iconography must express the faith of the Church and therefore is a highly theological art.

II. Orthodox iconography is an *eschatological* art.

Our second key adjective modifying iconography comes from the Greek word *eschaton* and designates "that which comes at the end." In a Christian context, it means the end of time, the Second Coming of Christ, that is, the Kingdom of God. For Christians, eschatological "time" and "space" are our time and our space transfigured by the glory of Christ. We use quotation marks to speak of time and space for the following reason: since our words describe the reality of our world, they lose some of the relevance when we try to talk about what goes beyond our experience of the world. This is why poetry, parables, and image language are better suited for talking about the end time than discursive, rational, scientific language. All the eschatological passages of the Bible, especially those of Daniel and Revelations, use verbal imagery that seems, to our far-too-earthly eyes, very close to pure fantasy. Let us recall Revelation 21 concerning the New Jerusalem:

> Then I saw a new heaven and a new earth; for the first heaven and the first earth had passed away, and the sea was no more. And I saw the holy city, new Jerusalem, coming down out of heaven from God ... . Then came one of the seven angels ... and showed me the holy city Jerusalem coming down out of heaven from God, having the glory of God, its radiance like a most rare jewel, like a jasper, clear as crystal... . The city lies foursquare ... . The wall was built of jasper, while the city was pure gold, clear as glass. The foundations of the wall of the city were adorned with every jewel ... jasper ... sapphire ... agate ... emerald ... onyx ... carnelian ... chrysolite ... beryl ... topaz ... chrysoprase ... jacinth ... amethyst. And the twelve gates were twelve pearls, each of the gates made of a single pearl, and the street of the city was pure gold, transparent as glass... . And the city has no need of sun or moon to shine upon it, for the glory of God is its light, and its lamp is the Lamb.

We can easily see that every word that tries to express the reality of the Kingdom of God must necessarily be deformed and stretched toward imagery so as to perceive "in a mirror dimly" (1 Cor. 13:12) that which we only know by foretaste. The same conditions apply to the icon but are expressed in a different manner: the icon has the task of representing, making visible, people and events in the light of the Kingdom of God. Such persons lived, such events took place in history, our history, according to the conditions that govern our existence, but they allow us to glimpse a reality which is not ruled by those conditions. Iconography, therefore, must use material and techniques that belong to our world (colors, lines, brushes, little colored stones, etc.) to show forth the

Kingdom of God. The icon's relation with the word is once again brought out: What poetry and parables are to the ear, iconography is to the eye.

Since the goal of iconography is to paint in the light of the Kingdom of God, where the old heaven and earth have disappeared and where all is new, it is not surprising that the iconographer should not try to reproduce the world as we know it on our side of the Second Coming of Christ. In this sense, iconography is not a "naturalistic" art whose *raison d'être* is to copy beautiful nature. Our world, finally, is not at all "natural" because it is deformed by sin and bound by death: two powers, conditions, that did not exist in the Garden of Eden are described in the first chapters of Genesis. Our human experience is set between two poles: the first one is the Alpha, "In the beginning ...," Paradise, where death and sin had no place, where Adam and Eve were naked and felt no shame, where the first parents did not kill to eat, where all was in harmony, where God and man spoke directly and lived in perfect communion. We should pay attention to the image language, the utopian description of Eden. Because we have no direct experience of this beginning, the biblical author was forced to reverse the conditions of our world in order to describe an existence about which we only have the vaguest intuitions. The second pole is the Omega, the end, "the End of Time," when Christ will establish his Kingdom in fullness—though again, we only have a foretaste of it.

In order to attain their objective, icon painters "twist" the principles of naturalistic painting (proportion, perspective, linear time, etc.) so as to suggest the irruption of a new reality into our world. Through iconographic techniques, the painter represents people, events, animals, plants, landscape, that we recognize as elements of our earthly existence, but which are nonetheless bizarre; they are arranged in a strange setting. It is by this strangeness that the icon indicates the newness of the heavenly Jerusalem, the Kingdom of God where we recognize our world, but not quite.

Several examples can help us see the tension between the necessity of representing the Beyond with the means of the Here-and-Now.

The background of an icon

Normally the background of an icon should be painted in gold, real gold or a golden color. The person or event painted is represented already in the Kingdom, bathed in its light. Gold is the most shining color, the richest; it is that earthly matter that best reflects the brilliance of light. And since the heavenly Jerusalem, according to Revelations, is made out of "pure gold," and having "no need of sun or moon to shine upon it, for the glory of God is its light," it is quite proper for the background of an icon to be of a golden color so as to reproduce the effect of being immersed in a blinding light. A golden background also establishes an unlimited framework in which the persons and events are set. It gives the impression that the subjects in the image are not in a spatial and temporal setting but rather float in a transspatial and transtemporal milieu. A naturalistic, realistic background would eliminate the sense of the presence of the divine light; the breaking through of the Kingdom into our world would be diminished.

The tendency of some contemporary iconographers to paint a black background, or one so dark in color that the psychological effect is the same as black, must be seriously challenged. Black is the color of death, sin, and darkness and diminishes the blinding effect of light. We have yet to hear a convincing justification of this tendency of substituting the brilliance of God's Kingdom for the somberness of Satan's.

Transspatial space

According to the principle of naturalistic painting,

the proportions and perspective of our world should be reproduced as faithfully as possible. If not, the public thinks it is looking at a surrealistic or symbolic work. A person in an icon, on the other hand, does not have the normal proportions of a human body. He is "stretched" and "thinned out" so as to increase the impression of being without weight or volume; nonetheless, the figure is clearly a human being, a man or a woman. We can easily identify buildings, trees, rocks, animals, etc., but they are different. If in nature as we know it lines come together as they move toward the horizon—railroad tracks, for example—the lines of perspective in an icon are often inversed and seem to come together in front of the image, in the person who is looking at the icon. (Several kinds of perspective may also be combined in one image.) The observer becomes the observed; the person in the icon is really the one doing the looking. In our earthly space, we normally look at paintings, but in heavenly space, into which the icon is a window, we become the object of someone else's gaze.

Transtemporal time

Linear time to which we are all accustomed—that is, the present following the past and preceding the future, a movement that allows no exceptions—loses its tyranny over us in iconic time. Two events separated in historical time can be shown on the same icon without any indication of temporal separation. The icon of the Protection of the Mother of God, October 1, combines two events in such a way that those who do not know how to read it think they are looking at one scene. In the upper two-thirds and in the lower right corner, we see St. Andrew the Fool in Christ and his disciple Epiphanius (Constantinople, 10th century) as well as the apparition of the Virgin seen by them[5] (fig. 3). In nearly all the space of the lower third of the icon, we see Romanos the Hymnographer (6th century) who is shown singing and directing

Figure 3 — The Protection of the Mother of God

the choir. In the calendar, the two events are celebrated on October 1, and this explains why both events are shown on one icon. The Pentecost icon as well as that of the Ascension also have a transtemporal quality because they are as much theological as historical. In both, St. Paul is represented event though at the historical moment represented on the image he was not even Christian. Icons can sometimes "twist" history by including St. Paul because they are at the same time images of an historical even and theological images of the Church. In an

53

Figure 4 — Resurrection of Christ

image purporting to illustrate the New Testament text of Pentecost, St. Paul has no place, obviously. In an icon of Pentecost, however, whose base is the historical event but which also transmits a transtemporal, theological interpretation representing the inner life of the Church, he has an eminent place. In these two feasts, the theological element is added onto the historical base.

The Easter icon, eschatological image par excellence

It is rather rare, and a corruption of the canonical

Figure 5 — The Myrrhbearing Women at the Tomb

iconographic tradition, to have an icon of Pascha show-ing Christ coming out of the tomb[6] (fig. 4). An icon of the historical event of the resurrection shows the myrrh-bearing women going to the tomb where they meet a shining angel seated on the stone near the rolled up burial clothes[7] (fig. 5). The resurrected Christ is not rep-resented. The other traditional image of Pascha is the

Descent into Hell in which Christ, surrounded by Old Testament characters, raises Adam and Eve from their tombs. The event itself is rather that of Holy Saturday when Christ goes to the "land of the dead" to announce the resurrection, but in fact this icon shows the resurrection of all humanity at the end of time, not Christ's specific resurrection. What we celebrate in the flow of linear time, after 2000 years of history, is the resurrection of Jesus of Nazareth around the year 33 and represented in the image of the myrrh-bearing women who were also living in the succession of historical moments. As for us, we must wait for the future moment when Christ will come again. On the other hand, for those who are no longer in the flow of time, those who have died in Christ, who are in a state where everything is the eternal present, the historical resurrection of Christ is already the Resurrection of the eschaton, of the End of Time.

III. Orthodox iconography is an *ecclesial* art.

The word *ecclesial* refers to the nature of the Church, what expresses its nature, what has its roots in the very being of the Church. We can distinguish it from the word *ecclesiastical* which designates rather what deals with the Church's action in history and society. For example, if we set *ecclesial structure* next to *ecclesiastical structure,* we can see that the first concerns something that touches the very nature of the Church, something that does not change, or at least very little, in history or from culture to culture. The other expression is reserved for changing structures that the Church has established for its efficient functioning under specific conditions and at specific times. For the Orthodox, the patriarchal structure, as we know it today, is ecclesiastical. It has not always existed in its present form, and we can easily imagine that history could profoundly modify it in the future without undermining the nature of the Church itself. Catholics can say the same for the college of cardinals. Although this assembly has been judged useful for the Catholic Church at a certain moment in history, nothing prevents it from being greatly changed or even abolished one day. The episcopate, on the other hand, for both Orthodox and Catholics, but not for Protestants, is an ecclesial structure which makes visible an aspect of the Church's nature. The episcopate has, nonetheless, taken, and no doubt will continue to take, various forms in time and space. As a result, something can be both ecclesial and ecclesiastical at the same time, and it is not always easy to distinguish the two. The papacy is a good example. In reference to this institution, Orthodox and Catholics are not agreed how to distinguish the one from the other.

For Orthodoxy, iconography is an art of the Church, ecclesial, not because it is necessary to the nature of the Church, but because the Church expresses its nature in iconography; it is the Church which is the real painter of an icon. In iconography, the Church visually expresses itself in the same way that it expresses itself orally when the Holy Scriptures are read in the liturgy. As a place of communion with God and the saints—that is, a "theo-sphere" where the transfiguring energies of God are at work—the Church creates another sphere, the icon, where the faithful can enter into contact with the Kingdom of God and open themselves to its sanctifying power. It is not by accident, therefore, that icons are naturally found in a church, in the middle of the liturgical action, and when we see icons elsewhere than in a church, they are but an extension of the mystery of Christ in the world. Each icon, whatever its subject, makes the unique mystery of Christ visible and active; that mystery can be summed up in the following way: Christ came to find his image—mankind, real men and women—lost and held in the clutches of sin and death, to clean that image, restore it, and lead it back into his Kingdom.

We also use the term *ecclesial* in relation to the role of

iconographers. These persons, men or women, lay or clergy, married or monastics, are instruments of the Church, therefore ecclesial persons who exercise their artistic talents to make the mystery of Christ visible and active. An iconographer's vocation is ultimately not the expression of artistic talent, as is the case with other artists. Even though some iconographers may have great artistic talent, even though their icons may be masterpieces of art, their goal is not to become celebrities. In reality, it is to do like John the Baptist next to Christ: diminish, withdraw, give place. Because its iconographers are much more than simple illustrators of Bible stories or lives of the saints, the Church is always concerned about them. It wants to be sure that their lives, by their Christian quality, express the Gospel, that they are immersed in the communion of the Church, that they conform to the iconographic tradition, and that they set aside all personal fantasy in their painting. This is the ideal, naturally, toward which all icon painters should work. Ecclesiastical history has shown, however, that the historical Church itself has not always risen to the height of its own ideal, nor iconographers either. Certain ecclesiastical canons, especially from the Russian Church, draw attention to the much too human and sinful aspect of iconographers organized into cooperatives. For example, the master painter should not, through jealousy, stand in the way of a young and talented painter nor favor members of his own family, nor accept people without talent, nor draw the bishop's attention to the good work of an apprentice while passing it off as the work of his mediocre pet. And again, iconographers should refrain from all drinking, pillaging, and theft. These canons paint an image of the iconographers which, to say the least, leaves something to be desired. Despite their highly spiritual and sacred calling, iconographers teach us the lesson that the yeast of the Gospel has not yet totally raised the heavy dough of humanity.

IV. Orthodox iconography is a *canonical* art.

Whenever we speak of canons in Church history, we often mean the laws established by a Church authority to regulate Christian behavior, laws which must be obeyed to avoid penalties. There is another definition, more ancient, that sees in the word *canon* an ideal, a measuring rule, a model to which we compare everything we do and say. In the final analysis, there are very few laws which govern the art of the icon. The adjective *canonical,* as it is used to modify *iconography,* refers rather to the second meaning: a model. A canonical icon is therefore an image that conforms to an established model of such and such a saint or event. Through the history and practice of the iconographic art, a tradition has been formed and has established models that artists are supposed to follow. Within the limits set by these models, painters are free to exercise their creativity.

Iconography is sometimes criticized by those who say that icon painters are not real artists, that they are not free, and that there is no place for creativity, for personal inspiration. These reproaches are based on key words such as *free, creativity, artist,* etc. which are in fact very elastic in nature. They can be adapted very easily to various and sharply divergent philosophies of art. It is simply untrue that the iconographer is not free and that his creativity is suppressed. To say such things only shows a lack of understanding of the nature of iconography. Inspiration, creativity, liberty are present and active in an icon painter, but these characteristics express themselves within a canon, a framework, established models, and not outside them. A good, canonical icon is a new creation, a free expression of an established model. In order to produce it, the artist must use his inspiration, his talent, to translate the canon into a new artistic work. As in any other area of art, there are master painters, as well as mediocre and bad artists, but the canonicity of the icons does not depend on the personal talent of the artist. An icon is canonical if it conforms to the model of the event or the saint. It is more or less uncanonical to the extent that it diverges from the model.

What is the relation between beauty and canonicity? In theory, there is none. To be canonical, it is not necessary for an icon to be beautiful. It is of course desirable that a canonical icon be well-made, beautiful, but the faithful expression of the model does not depend on its beauty. In any case, beauty is defined by an aesthetical value judgment which expresses a philosophical conception of art. Such a judgment is also determined by the taste of a period or a country. The appreciation of beauty changes continually, but the canon of a particular icon resists change.

The features of certain persons have received a fixed form in the iconographic tradition: for example, SS. Peter, Paul, and Nicholas. These saints are identifiable by their faces and other well-known signs. For SS. Peter and Paul, these features are essentially the same as those we see on a medallion of the 3rd century in the Vatican Museum. We of course cannot prove it, but it is not totally inconceivable that this medallion preserves the real features of the two apostles. In every icon where Peter and Paul are represented, on icons of the Ascension and Pentecost, for example, we can identify their faces. St. Nicholas is not in the same category. His face is much more stylized but nonetheless recognizable to those who know the tradition.

Let us look at some feast icons: Christmas, for example. It is sometimes said that St. Joseph and the midwives on the bottom third of the icon are optional features. They can be eliminated without great harm being done to the icon. In reality, Joseph—old, set apart, filled with doubt, sometimes tempted by a figure dressed as a shepherd (the devil)—represents the reaction of the fallen world to the event of a virgin birth. Joseph doubts but accepts the event nonetheless even though his reason cannot understand it. The midwives wash the baby. What newborn does not need to be washed? The presence of the midwives, washing the baby, proclaims that the Word of God is born in a completely human way, thus excluding any belief that would deny the full humanity of the incarnate Word. Such a tendency is called Docetism: the Word only *appeared* to be human, from the Greek verb *dokeo* meaning *to appear*. Therefore, an image of the Nativity of Christ that does not show Joseph and the midwives is not a canonical icon; it deviates from the established model.

We must avoid thinking, however, that absolutely everything in iconography has been established by the canon. The painter is free to paint many elements of an icon according to his imagination, as long as he remains faithful to what has been established. For example, there is no canon for a horse or for other animals. Each country and age has represented horses according to its experience of this animal. If we know how to distinguish different types of horses and their equipment, we can more easily determine the place and time of a particular icon. The art of the icon is therefore a combination of fixed elements, which the iconographer is obliged to paint according to the model, and unfixed elements, which the artist is in great measure free to represent as he wills.

V. Orthodox iconography is a *historical* art.

Although there are some legends claiming that certain images fell from heaven, what we recognize today as canonical iconography is the result of a long historical evolution. The iconographic tradition is in fact multifaceted, that is to say that it has changed and developed through time and that many peoples and civilizations have molded it. Local traditions have emerged and disappeared; "schools" have spread their influence, prospered, and finally faded away. The broad iconographic tradition is therefore a cluster of currents both diverse—from the point of view of style, origin, mediums, techniques, etc.—but united by their general orientation, by their vision that goes beyond simple techniques and mediums.

Since real, historical people have painted icons, these paintings legitimately lend themselves to the scientific study of art historians, Christian or otherwise; from this point of view, icons are like any other art form. It is not surprising then to note that Soviet art historians, atheists though they were, carried out some very good studies on icons.

We can once again draw attention to the parallels between icons and written documents: there are many styles of literature, many genres influenced by various eras, classical authors, different countries, etc., and specialists analyze all these in their scholarly studies.

We can identify several general historical stages in the evolution of iconography: a) before Constantine, 33-315; b) from Constantine to iconoclasm, 315-726; c) iconoclasm, 726-843; d) from iconoclasm to the fall of Constantinople, 843-1453; e) from the fall of Constantinople to the 20th century, 1453-1900; f) the 20th century.

A. Before Constantine: 33-315

In the first three centuries of Christian history, figurative art made its nearly unperceived entry into the life of the Church. Even though the Jews of the Old Testament, as well as of post-Biblical times, did not wildly give themselves to the development of a figurative art, like the Greeks, it is incorrect to say that they always rejected all images. Biblical history and the history of Jewish art contradicts this old, but false and tenacious, notion. However, as the early Christians moved out of their Jewish environment to preach to the Greco-Roman world and as they became more and more conscious of the implications of the doctrine of the Incarnation—that God became man—they began to enlarge the category of non-idolatrous images that were already present in their Jewish tradition. Our knowledge of this period is rather thin, but we know, nonetheless, that at the end of this first period, on the threshold of the Christian Empire, Christians had already begun to express their faith by symbolic images: the Good Shepherd, for example, and other images, even portraits and illustrations of historical people and events of the Old and New Testaments. We unfortunately do not know the name of the first Christian who painted the first Christian image; we have no idea either of the location or date of this event. We do know, however, that during this period, Christians undertook to adopt and adapt figurative art as a means of expressing their faith.

B. From Constantine to iconoclasm, 315-726

Between the Emperor Constantine and the iconoclastic crisis which began around 726, the Church found itself "married" to the empire. Christianity had become a state religion. Christian art, which up to that time had evolved slowly and without any guidance, was taken in hand by the empire and used as a political instrument. The Christian emperors needed buildings and churches worthy of their new place in the Church. Constantine, as well as other emperors, built monumental churches and properly decorated them with all kinds of images. The Church itself promoted the veneration of martyrs at their tombs where the faithful could often see a portrait, an icon, of the saint. The celebration of a cycle of feasts, such as Christmas, Annunciation, Transfiguration, etc., as well as a great number of new, non-martyr saints, required new images. Thanks to rich patrons, both emperors and other highly placed persons, artists adopted new mediums, such as mosaic. The confirmation, by the third ecumenical council (Ephesus, 431), of the title *Theotokos,* Mother of God, for Mary, gave a new vigor to the development of images of Mary. Finally, the Church adopted the pre-Constantinian, imperial art as well as other classical forms of Greco-Roman culture to its own needs. For example, the images of Christ and Mary enthroned, like emperors, took their place in iconography; the icon of the Nativity of Mary is partially a transposition into a Christian context of a general birth-scene, one that was well-known to antiquity: a woman lying on a bed, surrounded by midwives, with the baby being washed in a lower corner. The classical, canonical forms of certain icons began to appear in this period without, however, attaining their definitive form.

Near the end of this period, in 692, at the Quinisext Council, the Church officially expressed its preference for historical images over purely symbolic ones. The symbolic images of Christ as the Good Shepherd or the lamb were henceforth to give place to the direct image of the incarnate Word, Jesus Christ of Nazareth. Consequently, it is very rare to see Christ represented as a lamb in an Orthodox Church.

C. Iconoclasm, 726-843

There are four divisions in the iconoclastic period: 1. a very brutal opening period from 726 to 780 during which three emperors attempted to eliminate all icons from the churches; 2. an iconodulic lull from 780 to 813 when emperors in favor of icons defended them and tried to repress iconoclasm. (It was in this period that the Empress Irene called the 7th Ecumenical Council of Nicaea, 787); 3) the second, though less violent, iconoclastic period from 813 to 842 when emperors again tried to discourage the painting and veneration of icons; and 4) finally in 843, the Empress Theodora's liquidation of the anemic and moribund iconoclasm movement. A council was held in 843 in Constantinople which reestablished once and for all the orthodoxy of icons and their veneration. This victory is celebrated each year on the first Sunday of Lent as the Triumph of Orthodoxy.

D. From iconoclasm to the fall of Constantinople, 843-1453

During this period, the development of the icon reached its summit, and the canons, that is, the models, of various icons were fixed. The most important event from the artistic point of view is the transfer of this magnificent artistic heritage to the new missionary lands of the Slavic North. At the time of the baptism of Kievan Rus, 988, and throughout the following centuries, the new converts had only to assimilate what they received and then to begin producing a new variety of icons, at the same time faithful to the tradition but non-Greek in style. This is in fact just what they did. The Russian and Ukrainian tradition is the result, and, according to some, it has no rival as an expression of the spiritual vision that underlies the icon.

E. From the fall of Constantinople to the 20th century, 1453-1900

The fall of Constantinople to the Turks in 1453 put an end to the Christian Empire, except in its Russian version, and inaugurated a long period of hesitation and drift, even corruption, of the iconographic tradition. In Western Europe, another artistic vision was beginning to penetrate the minds and hearts of Christians, an evolution that would result in a complete rupture with the common vision of the past. The spirit of the Renaissance was already replacing the last expression of the iconography shared by East and West: Romanesque art. Even though we must recognize that the painters and sculptors of the Renaissance executed many artistic masterpieces, these artists decided to travel a road other than that of traditional iconography. The conquest of the East by Islam reduced the Christians there to poverty on all levels, but especially on the cultural level, and made Russia the only free Orthodox country. The poverty of the Orthodox and the wealth and power of Western countries produced in Eastern Christians an inferiority complex so that they saw everything coming from the West as superior to their Orthodox tradition. Historians speak of "the Western captivity." This mentality in the domain of iconography resulted in the popularity of Western images. The artistic vision of the Renaissance thus began to rival the theological vision expressed by icons to such a point that in the 18th and 19th centuries canonical iconography was nearly completely abandoned both in the Greek as well as in the Slavic worlds.

F. The 20th century

"... nearly completely abandoned" is in fact a very good expression to describe the situation at the end of the 19th century and the beginning of the 20th. At this period, the Spirit began to blow on the dry bones causing a renewal not only of canonical iconography but also of other aspects of the authentic Orthodox tradition. The result is the renaissance we are living today. We have once again become aware of the theological foundations of the iconographic vision, and we can measure to what degree an art based on another vision has dimmed the splendor of the icon.

Canonical iconography is therefore a historical art that has produced icons of many "styles": Greek, Russian, Ukrainian, Bulgarian, Arabic, Coptic, Ethiopian, Georgian, etc. For good or for bad, each period and country shaped this sacred art, and despite the ups and downs of history, the theological vision of the icon has always found a diversity of forms and expressions. It is therefore quite possible to hope that new, canonical icons, carrying the marks of the 20th century but faithful to the tradition, will be produced in our time.

VI. Orthodox iconography is a *sacred* art.

The opposite of sacred is profane. In order to have something sacred, there must be profane things. The two opposites go hand in hand. Our contemporary, Western culture defines itself, among other criteria, by the abolition of these two poles. Experts call such a culture "secularized," that is, one that defines itself without any reference to a reality or a truth that goes beyond the world that the empirical sciences can study. A society impregnated with a secularized vision simply does not recognize the existence of one of the two poles: the sacred. Everything is profane; therefore, nothing is profane, nothing sacred. From this point of view, the sacred/profane distinction has no meaning for human life. Even for many contemporary Christians, talk about the entirely-other-One, God, is colored by this secularized vision of existence.

Now in this cultural context, the icon reintroduces the sacred into our world. The problem is that the word *sacred* is very elastic, and it can carry many meanings. Many things can claim to be sacred: idols, prostitutes, the Bible, a mountain, a flag, the family, etc. Greco-Roman paganism, in fact nearly all kinds of paganism, established a link between our empirical world and the divine. The pagans of antiquity felt the presence of this other world but didn't advance very far in defining it. The link connecting the two worlds was an intermediate state of much-too-human gods and goddesses, priests and priestesses, sibyls, theophanies, sacrifices, and other mechanisms. Christianity, at its beginning and ever since, felt very uncomfortable in this sacred world because, from the Christian point of view, what is important is not some vague awareness of the sacred, but rather the very clear knowledge of the God of Israel. In the final analysis, the Greeks and Romans attacked Christianity for being atheistic because the Christians refused the sacred world of the gods.

Our contemporary cultural context is the reverse of that which prevailed in the first centuries of Christian expansion: our society has abolished everything sacred, and the icon bears witness to a presence whose roots are in non-empirical reality. However, the presence to which Church tradition witnesses, which the icon shows forth in lines and colors, is not the vague, imprecise, sacred world of antiquity. The icon does not open up just any sacred world; it gives us access very clearly to Him who is the source of all "sacrality," who spoke to Moses, who became incarnate in the historical person of Jesus of Nazareth, who makes himself known in the Church—even though Christian men and women often obscure that knowledge—who is waiting at the end of time to judge the living and the dead.

Even though our culture is becoming more and more secularized, we must not believe that people are thereby less hungry for God. The spread of sects, the multiplication of gurus, the fashion for esoteric philosophies, the fascination with cults, all this shows that our contemporaries refuse to define themselves in strictly materialistic terms. This refusal has its roots at a level of our being that is often little-known, ignored, or denied. People are still hungry, and a great number of preachers are offering food to the starving, food, however, that is tainted. There are even those who, in the name of the "sacred," use icons to express a syncretistic and esoteric religion; for those who advocate this point of view, icons do not announce Christ crucified, but are read as a statement of mystical "sacrality" or a gnostic philosophy completely detached from the God of Israel. A recent book, *Icons and the Mystical Origins of Christianity*,[8] represents this tendency, in fact the same one that St. Irenaeus of Lyons denounced in his *Against Heresies*. The phenomenon described by St. Irenaeus, among others, concerned the Carpocratians, a Gnostic group of

the 2nd century, who used images of Christ and the phi-
losophers in their worship (see *Against Heresies* I, 25, 6).
It is not surprising then—disturbing, yes, but not surprising—to see that people are taking advantage of the
popularity of icons, using them for their own purposes,
and impose on icons a message that is foreign to what
they authentically announce. And the most surprising
of all, the public, including Christians, does not have the
means to evaluate the truth of what is said in the name
of icons. Due to the absence, even banishment in some
circles, of any serious discussion about God in our contemporary culture, those who are hungry jump, without
any reflection, at the first "religious" thing that comes
along, at anything that gives the impression of being
"spiritual." Their unreflective choice often leads to their
destruction.

This cultural phenomenon obliges us to restate the
necessity of maintaining the close connection between
the icon and the Church community that produced it.
The more the icon drifts away from its source, the Orthodox Church, and from its authentic message, the Gospel of Christ, the more it loses itself in the religiosity of
the sacred. Iconography is indeed a sacred art, but a sacred *Christian* art, closely tied to the Bible, to Christ, to
the Church's tradition. Any other so-called sacred message which does not have its source there shows that it
comes from a spirit other than that of the Gospel.

As in all other areas, we need to be "informed con-
sumers" of the sacred.

VII. Orthodox iconography is a *mystical* art.

The words *mystic, mysterious, mystery* bring to mind
something hidden but at the same time exposed, at least
partially. Something that is absolutely hidden is absolutely unknown, and anything absolutely known has
nothing to reveal. In the two cases, mystery is impossible.

The icon is an image of mystery because it places itself between the hidden person depicted, that is, Christ or a saint, and the persons looking at the image, namely us. It is thus the vehicle of a personal presence that we feel but that we cannot grasp. To speak of a Christian mystery requires the use of two verbs: to be and to act. *To be* is needed because it makes present a person who is, who exists. On Mount Sinai, Moses met the Existing-One, God, the supreme mystery. A mystery also requires the verb *to act* because the Existing-One acts. He acts to attain an objective. An icon therefore participates in mystery to a great degree; it is a carrier of mystery—the technical word is *mysterophorus* —because it puts us in contact with a presence that can bring about a change in our lives.

The source of this active power is above all the human face. Even in the Old Testament, when God had no real face, the Bible often speaks of God's face to indicate a personal encounter with the Existing-One. In the New Testament, this face, in the figurative sense, has taken on a real human face so as to make his presence even more intimate. Human intimacy develops in face-to-face meetings. Lovers penetrate into each other by looking into each other's eyes. And when the beloved is no longer present, an artificial face, a portrait, a photo, serves as a substitute; it is a reminder, as painful as it is joyous, of the beloved because it evokes feelings due to the absence of the beloved.[9] A picture of the beloved shortens the psychological distance between the absent one and the one suffering from the person's absence. In other words, the image makes the absent one present, partially. To see the face of Christ or one of his friends in an icon also makes that person present, makes the mystery of that person present.

On the other hand, no one is blinder than he who does not want to see. No one is more untouchable by the mystery of the icon than he who does not want to be touched. There is nothing magical about an icon. If we choose to ignore the presence, if we close our hearts to its active power, Christ can do nothing in us. Therefore, although the person represented in the icon is really present and active, the refusal of the spectator can "neutralize" the mystery, or at least its effectiveness in that person; result: no change takes place. But what is this change that the mysterious, personal presence can bring about in us? Nothing less that the salvation of the one who looks, and, through him, the salvation of the whole creation. The icon is only another means, like the sacramental mysteries, of accomplishing Christ's grand plan of establishing the Kingdom of God.

Where is the icon's natural environment? What is the setting of which the icon is the gem? Since the icon itself is a place of communion where the mystery of Christ operates, it is natural that it should find its home in a place where the presence of that mystery is the densest: in the eucharistic liturgy, in a church. Everything that operates on the same wave length with the divine energies so as to receive and to retransmit God's "radio signal" is concentrated in the liturgy. The whole creation is therefore there present: architecture, music, painting, human voices, writing, incense, oil, bread, wine, and, finally, men and women. Since the liturgy is the place where the mystery of Christ operates the most intensely, it is not surprising that in this very place, we find the portraits of those who have allowed themselves to be transformed by Christ and to live in the Kingdom of God. Other places where we find icons are finally places linked in one way or another to the eucharistic liturgy: private chapels where a few faithful pray in communion with the whole community of believers; homes where a small ecclesial community, a Christian family, lives; cemeteries where the faithful, on the other side of death, wait for the coming of the fullness of the Kingdom; in nature where heaven's dome replaces that of the church and from which Christ Pantocrator watches over his creation.

Is there a relation between the fact that icons are two-dimensional and their mysterious nature? Why do three dimensional statues not have a place beside paintings? We have said earlier that a mystery that is too known and graspable lessens its mystical character. It is precisely the difference between two-dimensional and three-dimensional art that makes icons more appropriate carriers of the mystical sense. We can grasp and literally hold a statue. Behind a statue is more of the same kind of space that is found in front of it. A statue is surrounded by our space, the space of our world, the same space that surrounds us as well as the trees and the most ordinary objects of our daily lives. We do not want to say that a statue of Christ or of a saint is incapable of carrying a mystical sense, but according to the principles that govern iconography, a three-dimensional image in a three-dimensional world is too much like that world to allow the light of the Kingdom to shine through. A statue is time and space bound. On the other hand, a two-dimensional icon is already a twisting of our here-and-now reality since it projects a three-dimensional world onto a two-dimensional surface without worrying about the rules of so-called natural proportion or the ordinary flow of time. This kind of image opens up an uncapturable depth "behind" the surface and thus facilitates the irruption of the transfigured world of the Kingdom of God. At the most, bas-relief wood or metal sculptures have a place beside icons, but two-dimensional images remain the most capable of being vehicles of mystery, *mysterophorus.*

VIII. Orthodox iconography is an *ascetic* art.

Christian asceticism, in its healthiest expression, strives to make the spirit govern the body, to make the heart dominate the unruly and disruptive passions of man, and to reorient him who is a spirit-matter composite, toward the Kingdom of God. The word *ascetic* often has a bad reputation because, in the mind of many, it expresses a scornful attitude toward matter and the body. In truth, we are not without examples of Christian writers who have understood Christian asceticism as precisely the elimination and the destruction of the vital human forces instead of the reordering of their operation. The Platonic temptation of opposing spirit and matter, the material senses and the non-material intellect, has always been a diabolical temptation for Christianity. However, the creation of man as a composite being and the Incarnation of God the Word—in matter—make Church tradition allergic to this anti-biblical mind set. The Bible expresses rather a vision of the transfiguration of the whole creation, matter as well as spirit, all the dimensions of the cosmos, into the Kingdom of God. Such a vision implies, obviously, that the vital forces of man be directed toward God and not toward the earth, not turned in on themselves. Christian asceticism is therefore the activity, the struggle, the battle that aims at reorienting man and his energies upward.[10]

The icon expresses this vision 1) through the artist, 2) through the icon itself, and 3) through the observer. First the artist, the iconographer. We can suppose that the person painting the vision of transfiguration is living it or, at least, is in the process of living the struggle that leads to the ultimate goal. The iconographer, man or woman, must submit himself to the purification of his own vital forces. He must efface himself, "decenter" his life from himself (egocentrism) and "recenter" it on God (theocentrism). He must learn to eat in order to live and not live to eat. He must be chaste in marriage, in monasticism or in celibate life. In the three cases, the sexual energy, which pushes us toward union, must be oriented directly onto God or indirectly on him, passing through the consecrated union with one's partner in marriage. By becoming himself more and more transparent to the mystery, the iconographer sees that his art is also transformed. What he lives is projected onto boards in the forms and colors of his icons; his works reflect not only the struggle against the deregulated forces of his being but also the fruit of that struggle: inner peace, self-mastery, the proper functioning of all the elements, components, and dimensions of human existence.

The iconographer does not paint just to express his talent. He does not paint to make himself known. It is a deformation of the tradition to sign icons on the painted surface as if the artist wanted to make his work into just another painting. Even though such and such an artist may become known for the quality of his work, he should not seek fame as the ultimate goal of his artistic activity.

The icon itself gives off an odor of asceticism. It makes us feel the presence of a world and of persons who are calm, at peace, sober, restrained. All interior and exterior agitation is absent. The icon gives the impression that the men and women portrayed are stretched out; the proportions of the body are exaggerated vertically. Sensuality is reduced, and the accent is put on interior, spiritual beauty rather than on physical beauty. When we compare icons to Greco-Roman art, for example, we immediately feel the different energies of the two worlds.

On the icon of Pentecost, we see the apostles and the evangelists in a circle. They appear to be calm as if peacefully talking to one another. On the other hand, the New Testament tells us that on Pentecost, the disciples were so agitated that many people thought they were drunk. The icon of Pentecost does not show what the passers-by saw from the outside but rather, from the inside, shows the consequences of the reception of the Holy Spirit. We see on icons our world, not such as it is now—dislocated, divided, agitated, passionate—but as it will be in the Kingdom of God, and as it is in the process of becoming through Christian asceticism: calm, ordered, balanced, harmonious.

Finally, the observer is touched by the ascetic vision of the icon. We say "observer" to employ a neutral term because all of us do not necessarily feel invited to enter into the world of the icon just by looking. The icon does not have magic powers to force the observer to enter into its world. Everything depends on the heart of the observer, precisely as in the case of listening to a sermon or a Scripture reading. If the heart is not disposed to receive the message of the icon, nothing can force a person to receive it. Nonetheless, the icon can exercise an unconscious influence on the observer because there are many doors into the heart, and although some are well-guarded and impervious to God's grace, there are other levels, other doors, left standing unguarded and ajar. If the observer has the slightest opening to God, he can feel the icon's call and be pulled closer to him. Sooner or later, however, each person must decide to exercise his will and cooperate or resist the pull. It is at this point that human self-determination comes into play. The icon shows the great respect God has for our freedom. It calls us, invites us, attracts us into its ascetic world, but Christ through the icon requires a conscious decision for or against pursuing the transformation of the observer's life.

IX. Orthodox iconography is a *pedagogical* art.

The 20th century has largely been the century of the image. Photography, the movies, publicity all bear witness to the communicative and didactic power of the image. Popular wisdom has always known that an image is worth a thousand words, and the Church learned very early that images are effective as teaching aids. The word *teacher* and all the words in the same family evoke the idea of passing knowledge to those who do not have it, of

developing a competence in apprentices. It is a less eru-
dite word than *pedagogue* or *professor*, but the meaning is
the same. Images in the Church have always played the
role of instructing the faithful: the "Bible of the illiterate"
is a commonplace for everyone. One of the first written
testimonies to this principle comes to us from Italy,
around 400, when St. Paulinus of Nola explained that the
illustrations of Old Testament stories painted on the
walls of his basilicas were intended for peasant pilgrims:
"Everyone is aware of the crowds which Saint Felix's
fame brings here. Now the greater number among the
crowds here are country folk not without belief but un-
skilled in reading."[11] We must not think, however, that
images teach only the illiterate. The 3rd canon of the
Council of Constantinople, 869-870, says the following:
"We ordain that the holy icon of our Lord be venerated
in the same way as the book of the Gospels. Indeed, just
as all receive salvation through the syllables contained in
it, so do all, both learned and ignorant, draw profit from
what the colors of the icon possess... ."[12]

For learning to take place, three things are necessary:
1) a teacher who possesses 2) knowledge and who tries to
teach 3) students. Who is the teacher who instructs
through icons? As we have already seen before, iconography is an ecclesial art. It is therefore natural to assign the
teaching role to the Church which creates an atmosphere
in which the faithful can learn and which, by its centuries-old experience in making saints, passes on this
knowledge to the faithful. By the word *knowledge,* we
should not understand only pieces of historical information, whether doctrinal or spiritual. After 2000 years of
history, the Church has accumulated a library of names
and facts, and being acquainted with them, even curso-
rily, is important for any informed Christian. This type
of information is presented to the faithful, especially by
the icons of the saints or of feasts. The important events

of the lives of the saints are often painted on the edge of their icons. By listening to the liturgical hymns sung on the feast of each saint and by looking at the saint's icon set out in the church, believers can learn about the life of that particular person.

The teaching of the Church is not, however, uniquely carried out on the "academic" level but also on the experiential level. In order to attain the Kingdom of God, it is not necessary to be a historian, theologian, art historian, biblical exegete etc., in the scholarly sense of these terms. Those who carry out such studies have a gift from God which, like all other gifts, must be exercised to build the Church. But every believer has to be a theologian according to the meaning given that word by the patristic tradition: a person who has a knowledge (-logian) of God (theo-). The Christian is called to know God in prayer, nothing else, to be transformed by this knowledge, and to shine in the world by God's energies. The accomplishment of this vocation is open to all, whatever quantity of information one may have learned. Icons carry and teach this experiential type of knowledge as well as factual knowledge because they put us in contact with, in communion with, the person represented on the image. They open to us the possibility of learning and appropriating the "theological" experience of that person, that is, his or her state of deep prayer. Knowing facts about Christ or a saint and being in personal communion with them are two different, but complementary, things.

The third necessary element in the learning process is a student, either the believer, in this case, or ultimately every human being. We do not want to advance here the well-known distinction between the teaching Church—the clergy—and the learning Church—the laity. In the Orthodox patristic tradition, all Christians make up the Church, each one functioning in his role. No one has a monopoly on teaching in the sense that we have presented it here. All must learn to be saints; all need to receive lessons. The various hierarchical levels are not always coordinated with the learning, teaching, and developing of holiness.

X. Orthodox iconography is a *popular* art.

This word does not designate an essential aspect of the nature of iconography, but rather a phenomenon of our times. During many centuries, the art of the icon remained unknown to the West. After the Italian Renaissance had conquered the minds and hearts of Christians in Western Europe, the *maniera byzantina* was forgotten or, where known, was scorned because it did not conform to the naturalism in vogue at the time. In the 20th century, on the other hand, the popularity of icons continues to increase. We are living now in a time when icons are *à la mode*, popular.

There are advantages and disadvantages to this general interest in icons. In our contemporary society, in which God is more and more absent and in which everything is judged by its practical utility, the "bizarre" look of icons upsets some people due to their ability to call to the human soul on very deep, non-rational levels. The icon reintroduces a divine presence into everyday life. Icons can "sneakily" surprise nonchalant observers who have been anesthetized about an unsuspected dimension of their existence, a repressed dimension. The piercing eyes of a holy face penetrate the inner sanctum of "modern man," and there this face creates fear or peace. Even "secularized" Christians, if that is not a contradiction in terms, feel a joy or a malaise. The presence of God is a burning fire that either warms or burns the heart.

There is, however, the other side of the coin: we run the great risk of corrupting the tradition and of betraying the spirit of the icon. Since iconography is precisely an art, anyone who has some artistic talent can put brush to board and "produce" images. Icons are then reduced to a style: Byzantine, Russian, or other. They are produced and sold. The commercial temptation is very much alive in our times and mercantile hearts smell the wind and go after the promising market. It is even quite possible to order an "icon," that is, invent a subject, a person, that then becomes a kind of logo for such and such a cause. Certain artists care little or nothing about the Christian, Orthodox character of the icon. Their interest is strictly commercial.

At the other end of the gamut of motivations, we find people of good faith who decide to paint icons for themselves or for others without knowing what they are doing and without any preparation or direction; they are unaware, or only vaguely aware, of the highly sacred nature of this activity and its link with the Orthodox faith. The danger here is not commercializing the icon but making it banal, that is, reducing it to little more than a pious religious picture. These artists paint, sometimes through ignorance, sometimes knowingly, not according to the iconographic tradition nor in close collaboration with the ecclesial community but in private and too often according to their "phantasia." The results are innocent or disastrous according to the degree that they have deviated from the tradition. The reader should not assume that only non-Orthodox are meant here. The Orthodox also are ignorant of their own tradition or know it poorly and inaccurately. Finally, the greatest iconographic horrors have been painted by members of the Orthodox Church. Who invented St. Christopher with a dog's head[13] (fig. 6)?

The popularity of the icon, even though it may be but a passing fancy of the general public, contributes nonetheless to the artistic, historical, and theological research of the iconographic tradition's basic principles. In the final analysis, the tradition will be able to purify itself

Figure 6 — Saint Christopher with the head of a dog

and will not suffer greatly from its popularity. But after the "fad has faded," the canonical tradition will still be there to transform those who have eyes to see.

The ten words that we have used to describe canonical iconography do not constitute an exhaustive list, but we hope, nonetheless, that they deal with the essentials of this multi-dimensional art, thus deepening the reader's understanding of it.

NOTES

1. Eugene Trubetskoi, *Icons: Theology in Color*, Crestwood, NY, St. Vladimir's Seminary Press, 1973.

2. See (fig. 1) a Greek image of Joachim and Anne, 17th century, in the Eric Bradley Collection, #158, Temple Gallery, London, reprinted on card #158, St. Vladimir's Seminary Press, Crestwood, N. Y.; see the same image on the edge of an icon of Mary, in Gordana Babic, *Icônes*, Munich, Hasso Ebeling International Publishing, 1984, p. 52; see the sketch for December 9 in *An Iconographer's Patternbook: The Stroganov Tradition*, Ch. Kelley, tr., Torrance, CA, Oakwood Publications, 1992, p. 111.

3. See (fig. 2) an image printed by the Maison de Prière, Troussures, Auneuil, France, which reproduces the image "painted ... for the chapel consecrated to Mary and Joseph's marriage."

4. Bridge Building Images, Burlington, Vermont. The former name of the company was Bridge Building Icons and even at that time, the use of the word *icon* for some of the images presented was disquieting. Although the word *icon* is no longer used for every image sold, it still designates representations that do not conform to the tradition of the Church. The use of the word *icon* aside, the motivation behind the production of these images as well as the products themselves show that the Orthodox iconographic tradition has been used and misused for purposes at odds with its fundamental *raison d'être*. The fact that many people like, praise, and buy these images says nothing about the basic correctness of their production. It only indicates people's great lack of knowledge and gullibility.

5. Novgorod icon, end of the 15th century (fig. 3), L. Ouspensky and V. Lossky, *The Meaning of Icons*, Crestwood, N. Y., St. Vladimir's Seminary Press, 1982, p. 154.

6. See (fig. 4) a Greek image by Elias Moscos (1657), John Taylor, *Icon Painting*, New York, Mayflower Books, 1979, p. 77.

7. See (fig. 5) a Russian image of the 16th century, *The Meaning of Icons*, p. 189.

8. Richard Temple, *Icons and the Mystical Origins of Christian-*

ity, Dorset, UK, Element Books, 1990.

9. Euphrosyne Doxiadis, *The Mysterious Fayum Portraits: Faces from Ancient Egypt*, New York, Harry N. Abrams, 1995.

10. Jean-Claude Larchet, *Thérapeutique des maladies spirituelles* I & II, Paris, Les Editions de l'Ancre, 1991.

11. *The Poems of St. Paulinus of Nola*, Ancient Christians Writers 40, P. Walsh, tr., New York, Newman Press, 1975, p. 290.

12. S. Bigham, "Canons on Iconography," *The Image of God the Father*, Torrance, CA, Oakwood Publications, 1995, p. 128.

13. *Icon Painting*, p. 63.

Chapter 3

The Heroes of the Icon

I. Introduction

Iconography and holiness are closely related, as much by the object itself, that is the painted image, as by the person who produces it. The transfiguring mystery of Christ, which we can call "operating holiness," fills both. It is therefore very natural to expect that the Church would recognize certain iconographers as saints.

Saint Paul has this to say:

> Now there are varieties of gifts, but the same Spirit; and there are varieties of service, but the same Lord; and there are varieties of working, but it is the same God who inspires them all in every one. To each is given the manifestation of the Spirit for the common good. To one is given through the Spirit the utterance of wisdom, and to another the utterance of knowledge according to the same Spirit, to another faith by the same Spirit, to another gifts of healing by the one Spirit, to another the working of miracles … .All these are inspired by one and the same Spirit, who apportions to each one individually as he wills. (1 Cor. 12:4-11)

The troparion of the Transfiguration (a special hymn that announces the theme of the celebration) expresses the idea of a scale, a ladder of degrees, on which each Christian progresses toward the light of Christ according to his special gifts: "You were transfigured upon the mountain, O Christ our God, showing your glory to your disciples *as far as they were able to bear it …*" Certain icons of the feast make this notion visible in the different positions of the disciples' bodies after the theophany: the disciples fall down in the presence of the divine Light and cover their faces, but they do this in different ways, according to their individual ability to receive the vision.

These two ideas, diversity of spiritual gifts and individual progress toward holiness, are very naturally brought together in iconography. Even though St. Paul does not include artistic talent among his list of gifts, the Church through the ages has seen fit to recognize that this talent comes from God, and by glorifying certain exceptional artists, it has proclaimed that this gift allows artists to open themselves profoundly to God so as to reflect Him in their works as well as in their own lives. The result is a perfect marriage between a very personal, spiritual gift and the opening of the artist to God: in other words, a holy iconographer.

II. Prologue

A. Bezalel: Exod. 31:1-11

At the beginning of Israel's history as the people of the Law, we find the story of Bezalel, Oholiab, and other wise men who had received a gift from God for the execution of artistic works in the tent of meeting:

> The Lord said to Moses, "See, I have called by name Bezalel... I have filled him with the Spirit of God, with ability and intelligence, with knowledge and all craftsmanship, to devise artistic designs, to work in gold, silver, and bronze, in cutting stones for setting, and in carving wood, for work in every craft. And behold, I have appointed with him Oholiab...; and I have given to all able men ability, that they may make all that I have commanded you... ."

We have here a surprising association between artistic talent as a gift from God and the gift of God's Spirit. To accomplish their artistic work to the glory of God, certain persons are anointed with the Lord's Spirit. It is a sort of consecration, even ordination, that is necessary for artistic work done in God's name. This anointing with the Spirit for the doing of an artistic work is not essentially different from what the prophets received. In many passages, the Old Testament associates anointing with God's spirit and prophecy:

the 70 elders of Israel (Num. 11: 24-30)
Samson (Judg. 14:19)
Saul (1 Sam. 10:1-12)
the Servant of God (Isa. 42:1 and 61:1)
all flesh in the Messianic time (Joel 3: 1-6).

There is one Spirit but many gifts, and these gifts can lead to a high degree of holiness if the anointed one is obedient and exercises his talent for the glory of God. On the other hand, if the anointed one resists God—as Jonah did when he received the call to prophesy in Nineveh—or if he uses his artistic talent to make idols— as Aaron did when he made the golden calf—he will be condemned.

The witness of the Old Testament is therefore very clear: artistic talent is one of God's gifts, and by being anointed with God's Spirit, the artist can become a saint by using his gift to the glory of God. We should not be greatly bothered by the fact that the visual arts, artists, and their gift do not seem to have much importance in the Old Testament. The Israelites and the Jews apparently did not develop this gift as much as other gifts. Solomon had to hire a master craftsman from Lebanon, Hiram of Tyre, son of an Israelite mother and a Tyrenian father. 1 Kings 7:13-45 gives the impression that Hiram did all the work by himself, but according to 2 Chron. 2:15-5:1, Solomon had asked King Hiram of Tyre to send him a master craftsman. Hiram agreed and said that this man would "execute any design that may be assigned him, with your craftsmen, the craftsmen of my lord, David your father." It is not really important to know what proportion of the craftsmen were Jewish or foreigners. What is important is that the artistic gift given to both Jews and Gentiles is, according to the Scriptures themselves, a gift from God, a "sanctifiable" gift. The gift itself is rooted in Scripture. The flowering of this talent in the new people of God had to wait for another era, that of the Word of God incarnate: the era of the visible image of the invisible God.

B. Saint Luke the Evangelist: Luke 1-2

No one doubts that St. Luke the Evangelist was a doctor; St. Paul himself informs us of this fact in Col. 4: 14: "Luke the beloved physician and Demas greet you." But a tradition,[1] which is first spoken in a rather late, written document, indicates that St. Luke was also a painter. St. Luke supposedly painted the first icon of Mary and the Christ Child; its traditional name is the Hodogitria meaning "she who shows the way." Even if we can wonder about the historicity of this tradition, while still attributing, on the basis of piety, the first icon of the Mother of God holding the Christ Child to St. Luke, the choice of the third Evangelist is certainly not an accident. It highlights the close link that Church Tradition has always established between the word and the image.

At the beginning of his Gospel, St. Luke "paints" in words a detailed picture of Mary and the Christ Child. It is therefore completely logical to think that he was also a painter and to grant him the honor of having painted the first visible image of Mary and Jesus. The reputation of St. Paul's doctor friend does not rest, however, on his hypothetical artistic activity. St. Luke is first and foremost an evangelist, an artist of a verbal image of the Son of God's earthly life. His reputation for holiness is founded on something other than iconography even though the two are by no means incompatible.

Why have we put Bezalel and St. Luke in a prologue? In the first case, Bezalel represents a righteous man of the Old Testament. It is rare to call the people of the Law *saints.* Old Testament holiness is not the same as Pentecostal holiness. Before the coming of Christ and Pentecost, the Holy Spirit sanctified the men and women of Israel, as it were, from the outside; after Pentecost, however, the Spirit transforms men and women of the Church from the inside, in a way that is essentially different from the former type of sanctification. The Spirit continues to distribute his gifts, among which is artistic talent, but the potential is vastly enlarged. The artist can now paint the face of the Son of God himself; this was forbidden by the Law of Moses. An artist can now become an iconographer.

We have put St. Luke in the Prologue because of the fragility of the tradition that designates him an iconographer. Despite the internal logic of the piety on which the tradition is built, we prefer not to go beyond the limits of "according to tradition... ."

III. THE HOLY ICONOGRAPHERS

Here is a succinct description of an iconographer: "He consecrated all his time to prayer and iconography, thus expressing in lines and colors the fruits of his contemplation."[2]

1. Saint Lazarus the Iconographer of Constantinople (November 17: 810?-867)

Our father among the saints, Lazarus of Constantinople, is the first iconographer glorified by the Church. He was a monk and an iconographer who lived during and after the second period of iconoclasm (813-843). He is also counted among the confessors of Orthodoxy because, despite the persecutions that the lovers of icons had to undergo at that time, Lazarus continued not only to confess his faith but also to paint icons. In 856, after the defeat of the iconoclasts, the Emperor and Patriarch sent him to Rome to talk with Pope Benedict III about reestablishing peace and unity among the Churches. He died during a second trip to Rome in 867. His body was sent to Constantinople where he was buried in the monastery of Evandres near the city.

In the *Life of St. Lazarus*,[3] we read about the following virtues: love for Christ, asceticism, prayer, and rejection of the vanities of the world. These are qualities expected of all the faithful, but St. Lazarus' biography highlights another characteristic directly related to his life as an iconographer: He persevered "in *asceticism* and *prayer* so as to prepare himself to transcribe his inner contemplation onto the images that he painted...." We have here the perfect expression of the role of an iconographer, and of the icon itself, in the process of man's sanctification.

Let us examine the elements of this sanctification, that is, the upward movement toward God:

1) The life of a holy Christian is not built on a moment of illumination, a momentary explosion of energy, but rather on a long and difficult road. On this road, the Lord purifies, prunes, those whom he loves from everything that blocks and impedes the person's ascension toward Him. Perseverance is necessary in order to arrive at the end of the road. St. Lazarus persevered.

2) We have already seen that prayer and fasting are fundamental to the Christian life if we hope to expel certain demons. Asceticism is a constant war against the disorders created by powerful and irrational drives, that is, the passions, in the heart and mind of every person. Prayer, private or corporate, turns the conscience toward God, a conscience made up of thoughts, images, and words. By establishing tranquillity in the heart through asceticism, the Christian can more easily orient his spiritual antenna toward the divine energy emanating from God. The goal of this struggle is to prepare the Christian for inner contemplation. St. Lazarus practiced asceticism.

3) The word *contemplation* has a long history; it has many definitions and nuances and is also often misunderstood. In the context of this study, we can limit our-

selves to the following: according to the mystical vision of the Orthodox patristic tradition, contemplation is not limited to an exercise of rational and conscious thought. In its connotation, contemplation goes far beyond physical and mental looking, beyond examining an object or an event to discover its meaning for our life today. This is not excluded, but the ultimate goal is rather to open ourselves to God, let him invade our hearts, and to know and feel his burning presence in our inner being.

4) Up to this point, we have described the vocation of every Christian. According to the spiritual gifts of each person, the expressions of this mystical vision will be different. In the case of St. Lazarus, having received the gift of painting, he applied his talent so as "to transcribe his inner contemplation onto the images he painted." He exercised his gift by painting the vision of God in icons. As a result, the Church recognized in him and in his works of art an expression of the authenticity of the Christian spiritual life. St. Lazarus and his works manifested such an opening towards God that it is no wonder that his biographer speaks of the power of his intercession as well as of the miracles that God did through his icons. St. James tells us that "the prayer of a righteous man has great power in its effects." (Jas. 5:16) In Acts, we learn that "God did extraordinary miracles by the hands of Paul, so that handkerchiefs or aprons were carried away from his body to the sick and diseases left them… ." (Acts 19:11-12) Even though we must always be vigilant and eliminate corruption's that can too easily slip into the beliefs and practices of Christians, the Scriptures clearly say that the Lord can use persons and things to manifest His power. St. Lazarus the iconographer and his icons were just such instruments.

In our time, when many are asking themselves whether it is possible to heal the schisms among the Churches, it is interesting to note that the Byzantine

Church and State chose a holy painter to carry out two missions whose goal was precisely unity among the Churches.

2. Saint Alipy the Iconographer of Kiev
(August 17: 1078?-1114?)

See the Annex for the *Life of Alipy* and for the story of the arrival of the Greek iconographers in Kiev.[4]

At the very beginning of Christianity in Russia, we find a holy Russian iconographer associated with some Greek iconographers. The iconographic tradition had already reached its classical and canonical form in Byzantium after the iconoclastic controversy, and it was then carried in full bloom to Russia. The Russians had only to come to feast and participate. History has shown that from the start Russians have greatly delighted in the meal. Having adopted and developed the artistic treasure brought from Constantinople, Russian painters have done their Motherland proud showing themselves worthy of the gift they received.

We have, therefore, in the Russian painter Alipy a model of holiness that was transmitted to the Russian Church in the following centuries. Having a holy iconographer among its founders, the Russian Church has only needed to encourage talented, local artists to follow the example of one of their own "Fathers among the saints."

When we read the *Life of Alipy*, what do we learn about his character? What has Church Tradition preserved concerning this model of a Christian painter?

a) First of all, Alipy was an inspired imitator of St. Luke. On the basis of St. Luke's place in the iconographic tradition, it is not surprising that the Evangelist serves as an important model for all iconographers. However, here, the word *imitator* praises the saint and emphasizes the role of the artist in the Church: the iconographer receives, assimilates, reproduces, and transmits the iconographic tradition in a faithful way. He is not an innovator. Having said this, we must not understand, as is often the case, that creativity has no place in the faithful transmission of the art of the icon. The more the artist is immersed in the theological vision that the icon expresses, the more his innate talent will develop and the more the fruit of his work will be a new and original expression of that tradition.

b) Alipy represented the faces of the saints on icons; at the same time, his soul was filled with virtues. The *Life* brings out the relation between what Alipy possessed in his soul—holiness—and what he represented on the icons of the saints. We have this same idea expressed in the *Life of St. Lazarus of Constantinople* who transmitted to his icons his inner vision. Before being able to express the vision of holiness through painted images, the iconographer must know this holiness in his own inner spiritual life. As with every good iconographer, after a period of study and advanced training, Alipy was able to "represent on material images the spiritual virtues of the saints. The interpenetration of the spiritual and the material is characteristic of Orthodox spirituality and is clearly manifested here. Alipy was so deeply filled and transformed "by the grace of God" that he was able to project into matter, through colors and lines, the spiritual reality of the saints. Matter can be heavy and opaque, or it can be light and diaphanous. Alipy knew how to make holiness shine through matter.

c) Alipy's holiness made him not only a great artist but also "an amazing healer."

d) Alipy often painted free of charge. Money had little value for him. This is not surprising in someone who is oriented toward the Kingdom of God. Alipy exercised his talent not to become rich but "to develop his virtues." "He practiced virtue as he practiced his art." Matter cannot only reflect holiness; however, physical activity, the exercise of a profession—in this case iconography—can also be the vehicle that leads one up to God.

e) Alipy worked all the time; he was never idle. He was humble, detached, pure, patient, charitable, ascetic, and generous. These are all virtues that we see in all the saints, whatever their particular type of holiness.

3. Saint Gregory the Iconographer of Kiev, Alipy's companion (August 8: approximately the same dates as St. Alipy's: 1078?-1114?)

Vladimir Ivanov notes one person who does not appear in our *Life* of St. Alipy: a collaborator named Gregory, no doubt a Russian.[5] Ouspensky also mentions Gregory.[6] The *Life of Gregory* only says this: "August 8: the venerable Gregory, iconographer, wonder-worker of the Pechersky Monastery, companion of the venerable Alipy (11th century). The venerable Gregory's holy relics were placed in the cave near the venerable Antony."[7] We have not been able to find any other information on St. Gregory the Iconographer of Kiev. It is quite reasonable to assume that other young artists were trained in the iconography "school" of Kiev directed by Greek artists. Nonetheless, we have very little reliable information on this enigmatic person.

4. Saint Peter the Metropolitan of Kiev (December 21: 1308-1326)

See the Annex for the *Life of St. Peter*.[8]

The Chronicle of Novgorod speaks for the first time of Metropolitan Peter when he confirmed David as Archbishop of Novgorod in 1309.[9] In 1325, St. Peter participated in the funeral of Grand Prince Yuri. The *Chronicle* records his death in 1326: "Through his prayers God performed miracles at his tomb."[10] Tradition associates two icons with St. Peter: the *Savior with an Angry Look* and the *Petrovskaya Virgin*. The fact that the Metropolitan himself painted icons certainly gave a boost to the development of a Muscovite style. We have a confirmation of St. Peter's artistic activity in an icon painted in Dionysius' workshop at the beginning of the 16th century. Among the scenes of Peter's life shown on the edge of the icon, we find the Metropolitan being trained as an iconographer.[11] He died in 1326.

5. Saint Basil the Archbishop of Novgorod
(February 10: 1330-1352)

According to *The Chronicle of Novgorod,* Basil was named Archbishop of Novgorod in 1330 and consecrated in 1331.[12] His episcopate continued until his death in 1352. The Russian Church commemorates him on February 10 along with the other bishops buried in the Cathedral of the Divine Wisdom in Novgorod. Ivanov praises the period of Archbishop Basil in the following way: "With Archbishop Basil, religious and artistic life reached its height between 1330 and 1360; he was himself an icon painter."[13] Unfortunately, the *Chronicle* says nothing about Archbishop Basil's artistic activity. However, it associates him with Isaiah, a Greek iconographer, and his companions whom the Metropolitan hired to paint a church. It is certainly true that the Archbishop's name is related to the construction of many churches which, naturally, needed icons and frescoes. In the *Life of Archbishop Basil,* we read the following:

> St. Basil succeeded Moses—one of the most remarkable archbishops of Novgorod. He was a priest in the world whose name was Gregory Koleka. He built a wall around the city, built churches after the fire, and himself painted icons. Archbishop Basil fiercely defended the rights of his city. For his activities, the Patriarch of Constantinople sent him a white klobuk [normally a black, cylindrical hat covered by a veil and worn by monks and bishops] and other priestly vestments.[14]

6. Saint Theodore the Iconographer, Archbishop of Rostov
(November 28: +1394)

The *Orthodox Liturgical Calendar of the Orthodox Fraternity of Western Europe* gives Theodore the title of "iconographer."[15] The *Synaxarion*,[16] however, as well as the *Life*[17] of St. Theodore say nothing on the matter.

7. Saint Andrei Rublev (July 4: 1365?-1430?)

See the Annex for the *Life* of St. Andrei.[18]

We have very little information on the life of Andrei Rublev, but his influence on the Russian iconographic tradition cannot be denied. He was born between 1360 and 1370 near Moscow; we do not know the exact date. At a very young age, Andrei entered Holy Trinity Monastery where St. Sergius was still the hegumen. The historical documents that we have describe Andrei as a young monk at the time of Nikon, St. Sergius' successor. Before 1405, Andrei moved to the Spasso-Andronikov Monastery where he was tonsured. There he met Theophanes the Greek, his iconography teacher, as well as Daniel Chorny, his life-long companion. The *Life of St. Nikon* indicates that the two painters were "men perfect in virtues... ., virtuous elders and painters. They always lived in spiritual brotherhood having great love for each other... Thus, they went to God...in spiritual union as they had lived here on earth."[19] Another chronicle of the time has this to say:

> In the springtime of that year [1405], the stone church of the holy Annunciation in the Grand Prince's palace—not the one that is standing now— began to be painted. The masters were the Greek icon-painter Theophanes, the elder monk Prokhor from Gorodets and the monk Andrej Rublev. They finished in the same year.[20]

It is noteworthy that Rublev is mentioned in third place. At the time, he was no doubt young and relatively unknown. In 1408, Daniel Chorny and he painted the frescoes in the Dormition Cathedral in Vladimir. Epiphanius the Wise tells us that St. Andrei, by himself, painted the interior of the cathedral of the Merciful Savior in the Andronikov Monastery. A very realistic image of a Greek ship in the cathedral has led many specialists to think that Rublev may have spent time in Constantinople, but this is only speculation. St. Nikon, who built the Trinity-Saint-Sergius Monastery in 1422, asked Andrei Rublev and Daniel Chorny to paint the interior. We can suppose that at this time Rublev painted the famous icon of the Trinity. The *Life of St. Nikon* tells us that St. Andrei died around 1430 "at a very advanced, venerable, and honorable age." He was buried in the Andronikov Monastery that is now the Rublev Museum.[21]

Having sketched the lines of Andrei Rublev's life, let us now look at the following passage which indicates just how much his acts and works were an expression of his inner life. This passage reminds us of the *Life of St. Alipy* which also emphasizes the relation between the mystical experience of the divine Light and the representation of this Light on an icon:

> St. Andronik was aglow with great virtues. He had Sava and Alexander as disciples, along with the marvelous and famous iconographers Daniel with his disciple Andrei, and many others who resembled them. They were so full of virtue and showed such zeal for fasting and the monastic life that they were filled with divine grace. They prospered in divine love because they took no care for anything earthly; they always turned their minds and thoughts toward the immaterial and divine Light. They continually fixed their eyes on what had been painted in past centuries, that is, the image of God [Christ], the all-holy Mother of God, and all the saints. On the day of the luminous Resurrection of Christ, these painters, seated on their chairs, had before their eyes the venerable and divine icons looking at them without ever

turning away. It was at this moment that the divine joy and Light flooded into them. This is what they did, not only on that day but also everyday that they were not busied with painting. This is why Christ our Lord glorified them at their last hour. Andrei died first; then his companion fell sick. At his last breath, Daniel saw his companion Andrei in a cloud of great glory, and Andrei called to him with joy to come and join him in infinite and eternal happiness.[22]

Rublev's reputation for holiness and artistic quality was such that a century after his death he was still considered the model to be followed. In 1551, the Council of 100 Chapters (Stoglav), in its 43rd chapter, decreed the following: "Painters will reproduce the ancient models, those of Greek iconographers, Andrei Rublev, and well-known painters."[23] The Stroganov *Painter's Manual*, from the end of the 16th century, had already spoken of Rublev as a saint: "Holy Father Andrei of Radonezh, iconographer, named Rublev, painted many icons, all of them miraculous.... He was under the direction of Father St. Nikon of Radonezh who ordered an icon of the all-holy Trinity to be painted for the glory of his spiritual father, St. Sergius the Wonder-Worker ..."[24] The name of Andrei Rublev is written in certain old menologia, and quite a number of illuminated manuscripts show him with a halo.

Troparion, Tone 3

Resplendent in the rays of the divine Light, O Saint Andrei,
You knew Christ who is the Wisdom and the Power of God,
And by the icon of the Holy Trinity,
You proclaimed to the whole world the triune God.
Thus, standing in great wonder and joy, we cry to you:
You who have boldness before the Holy Trinity,
Pray that we too may be illuminated.

8. Saint Gregory Tatevatsi (1346-1409)

St. Gregory was a member of the Armenian Apostolic Church and directed a university at Tatev. He was a priest as well as a painter, copyist, musician, poet, philosopher, and theologian. A gospel (#7482) copied and illuminated by him can be found in St. Petersburg; he signed it in 1378. It is possible that he painted other manuscripts also, but he only signed and dated one of them. There is some controversy about another manuscript, #6305, that some specialists attribute to St. Gregory Tatevatsi, while others attribute it to an anonymous illuminator.[25]

9. Saint Dionysius, Hegumen of Gloushitsa (June 1: +1437)

See the Annex for the *Life of St. Dionysius.*[26]

Dionysius began his ascetical life in the Kouben Monastery, but wanting to live a solitary, hesychastic life, that is, one of interior tranquillity in the practice of the prayer of the heart, he withdrew into the forest near the Gloushitsa River. Despite his seclusion, he attracted more and more disciples who wanted to live the monastic life with him. Consequently, he had to transform his hermitage into a monastery. Dionysius was a talented iconographer, a coppersmith, and a stone cutter.[27]

10. Saint Dionysius of Olympus (January 23: +1541)

On the information given by N. Kalogeropoulos and by Photios Kontoglou, Phoibos Piompinos[28] calls St. Dionysius of Olympus an iconographer. We have not been able to confirm this information in any other source, including two Greek synaxaria. On the other hand, Father Macarius, the editor of the French synaxaria, has indicated that he possesses information that confirms the iconographic activity of St. Dionysius. We have therefore not included his *Life* in the Annex.

St. Dionysius had three principal activities: his

hermitic life, the spiritual direction of the brothers who came to him, and the instruction and consolation of the Christian people who, during this time, had great need of pastoral care. He was a monk on Mount Athos, in Jerusalem, and finally in the Mount-Olympus region where he died in peace in 1541 surrounded by the brothers of his monastic fraternity.

11. St. Macarius, Metropolitan of Moscow
(December 30: +1547)

Macarius was born in Moscow in 1482. At a very young age, he became a monk in the St. Paphnutius Monastery in Borovsk. There he learned the art of painting icons. In 1532, he was named Archimandrite of the Monastery of St. Therapont in Mozhaysk; in 1526, he was consecrated Archbishop of Novgorod and Pskov. He organized the life of the Church which had been in disarray for many years. He sent missionaries into the countryside around Novgorod to convert the native peoples of that region. He organized all the Novgorodian monasteries according to a single community rule and threw himself into the building and decoration of the churches in his diocese. Thanks to Archbishop Macarius, many of the workshops he founded were able to supply all the new churches with the goods and equipment they needed. In 1529, he conceived a great project: gather together and edit the *Lives of the Saints;* after 12 years, the *Minei Chetii* appeared. According to the chronicles, Archbishop Macarius was an "accomplished iconographer." In 1528, the saint restored the icon of the most-holy Mother of God, called the Sign that the passage of time had greatly deteriorated. Once the work was finished, his Excellency the Archbishop himself, surrounded by a great crowd of Novgorodians, had the icon of the Mother of God carried in procession to the Church of the most-holy Mother of God.[29]

In 1542, the Russian Church elected Archbishop Macarius Metropolitan of Moscow; he was 60 years of age. During his episcopate in Moscow, he began to print books in Russian. In 1555, on his own, he restored an icon of St. Nicholas. The chronicles say that "Metropolitan Macarius himself restored the icon of St. Nicholas the Wonder-Worker, for he was very accomplished in the art of icon painting…with much desire and faith, fasting and prayer."[30] At the age of 81, in 1563, Metropolitan Macarius fell asleep in the Lord and immediately became the object of the people's veneration.

We read the following passage in the *History of the Holy Iconographers:*

> The wonderful Metropolitan, St. Macarius of Moscow and of all Russia, wonder-worker, painted holy icons and wrote books and the *Lives of the Holy Fathers* for each day of the year, as well as the *Minei Shetii,* as no other Russian had done before him. He ordered the celebration of the feasts of the Russian saints; he put in force a rule for the cathedral; and he painted an image of the Dormition of the most-holy Mother of God.[31]

In a short *Life of St. Macarius* from the 17th and 18th centuries, the author makes no reference to the Metropolitan's artistic activity.[32] This information is found, however, in the document called *History of the Holy Iconographers.* It was therefore known that Macarius was a painter. It is strange, nonetheless, that in the first *Life of St. Macarius* no mention is made of his being an iconographer.[33]

12. Saint Adrian of Poshekonia (March 5: +1550)

St. Adrian was the hegumen of the monastery of the Dormition that he himself had founded in the forest of Poshekonia. He was also an iconographer. In 1550, thugs attacked the monastery and killed him.[34]

13. Saint Cornelius, Iconographer, and His Disciple, Saint Bassian of Pskov, Martyrs (February 20: +1570)

See the annex for the *Life of St. Cornelius*[35]
Cornelius was the hegumen of the monastery of the Caves of Pskov. He painted icons and decorated his monastery; he helped to educate the most talented of his novices in the art of the icon. Cornelius was also a missionary among the Latvians. In order to protect his monastery against attacks, he built a wall around it. Tsar Ivan the Terrible suspected Cornelius of seditious intentions and in 1570, in a great rage, the tsar killed Cornelius and his disciple Bassian. After the brutal act, Ivan realized what he had done, repented deeply, and honored Cornelius with an imposing tomb.[36]

14. Saint Ananias the Iconographer (June 17: +1581)

Ananias lived in the Novgorodian monastery of St. Antony where "he consecrated all his time to prayer and iconography, expressing through lines and colors, the fruit of his contemplation."[37] He died in 1581. Here is the short notice of his *Life:* "The venerable Ananias, monk of the Antoniev Monastery in Novgorod, was an iconographer and followed the monastic rule very strictly. During the 33 years of his monastic life, he never left his monastery."[38]

15. Saint Pimen of Zographou, or Sophia (November 3: +1610)

See the *Life of St. Pimen of Zographou* in the Annex.[39]
Pimen was born in the middle of the 16th century and at a very young age began to study iconography with a local priest iconographer. His life is divided into two periods. The first deals with the time he spent in the Bulgarian monastery of Zographou on Mount Athos where he continued to paint. The second began when Pimen decided to leave the monastery to shepherd his people who were without a pastor. His name Pimen means *shep-*

herd in Greek. After his return to Sophia at the age of 55, Pimen spent all his energy in pastoral work, building and renovating churches and monasteries. As an iconographer, he decorated many of them. His energy and devotion won him the grateful thanks of his people, and his art, that of painters. He is the patron of Bulgarian iconographers.[40] He died in 1610.

16. Anastasius the New Martyr of Nauplios, Greece (February 1: +1655)

Anastasius had the gift of icon painting. He was forced to break his engagement to his fiancee because of her unworthy behavior. The young girl's parents made Anastasius temporarily insane by the use of occult practices, especially drugs. During his delirious moments, the Muslims of the city circumcised him and dressed him in Turkish clothes. After having recovered his good senses, Anastasius refused his "conversion" to Islam and proclaimed his Christian faith before everyone. A court condemned him to death, but an enraged crowd killed him before the execution of the sentence.[41]

17. Saint Iorest, Metropolitan of Transylvania (April 24: +1657)

See the Annex for the *Life of St. Iorest.*

St. Iorest was a monk and talented icon painter in the Putna Monastery in Moldavia. In 1640, he assumed the post of Metropolitan of Oradea. St. Iorest fought for Orthodoxy against the Calvinists who were persecuting him. He was imprisoned in 1643, ransomed nine months later, and elected bishop of Chous in 1657. He died several months after his election.[42]

18. Saint Joseph the New Hieromartyr of Constantinople (No liturgical commemoration: +1819)

See the notice for St. Joseph in the Annex.[43]

St. Joseph was an iconographer and monk at the beginning of the 19th century. He suffered martyrdom because of the weakness of a brother monk, Evdokimos. Oddly enough, he has no liturgical feast.

19. Saint Savvas of Kalymnos, Monk and Iconographer
(April 7: 1948)

Savvas was born in 1862 in Thrace. At 28, in 1890, he became a monk at the Monastery of St. George Choziba in the Holy Land. To perfect his knowledge of iconography, he spent time at the St. Anne Skete on Mount Athos. When he returned to Choziba in 1907, Savvas intensified his hesychastic life in prayer and iconography. Around 1916, he met St. Nectarius of Aegina and entered into the service of the holy bishop. Savvas remained several years in Aegina where he was chaplain to a group of nuns to whom he taught iconography and chanting. After the death of St. Nectarius, Savvas painted the first icon of him, and it was placed in the local church for the veneration of the faithful. In 1926, Savvas retired to the island of Kalymnos where he spent his last 28 years taking care of his spiritual children and painting icons. He died on April 7, 1948.[44]

IV. The Holy Martyrs and Confessors of the Icon

Iconoclastic emperors (I) and Orthodox emperors (O)

The First Period of Iconoclasm
(I) Leo III the Isaurian 717-741
(I) Constantine V Copronymus 741-775
(I) Leo IV 775-780

The Iconodule Interlude
(O) Constantine VI 780-802
(O) Irene 797-802
(O) Nicephorus I 802-811
(O) Staurakios 811
(O) Michael Rangabe 811-813

The Second Iconoclastic Period
(I) Leo V the Armenian 813-820
(I) Michael II 820-829
(I) Theophilus 1829-1842

The Final Victory of Iconodulia
(I) Michael III 842-867

A. The First Period of Iconoclasm: 726-780

1. Theodosia the Martyr (May 29: +730)

When Leo III launched his iconoclastic campaign in 726-730, one of the first acts of violence was the destruction of Christ's icon on the Chalkis gate in Constantinople. Theodosia and some other women shook the ladder on which was standing a soldier who wanted to deface the icon. He fell off and was killed. The women then went to the palace and stoned Anastasius, the new iconoclastic Patriarch. For their audacious action, the women were beheaded, and Theodosia was stabbed in the throat. She died in 730.[45]

2. Julian, Marcian, John, James, Alexis, Demeter, Photius, Peter, Leontius, and Mary the Patrician (August 9: +730)

These ten martyrs died in 730 for having resisted the destruction of the holy icon of Christ on the bronze gate, called Chalkis, in Constantinople. At this date, the Emperor Leo III the Isaurian began his campaign against icons by destroying the famous image attached to the gate of the city. A riot ensued, and imperial soldiers killed many furious citizens among whom were numbered the ten martyrs mentioned above.[46]

3. Peter the Martyr (November 28: +730)

Peter was beaten to death because he continued to venerate the holy icons: "Peter was beaten for the holy images, but his body felt the blows as though he were getting a massage."[47]

4. Germanus the Patriarch of Constantinople, Confessor
(May 12: +733)

Germanus was the Patriarch of Constantinople who, for the first time, had to confront the iconoclasm unleashed by Leo III the Isaurian between 726 and 730. Leo tried to convince the Patriarch to support his anti-icon policy, but only in vain. With the support of Pope Gregory II, Germanus remained inflexible. A council dominated by the Emperor deposed Germanus, and Anastasius, a new iconoclastic Patriarch, took his place. Germanus died in 733, in exile on his family estates.[48]

5. Procopius of Decapolis, Confessor
(February 27: +8th century, exact date unknown)

Under the reign of the first iconoclastic Emperor, Leo III the Isaurian, Procopius was a fervent monk in Constantinople. By his words, acts, and suffering, he proclaimed that the veneration of icons is right and proper.[49]

6. Basil the Confessor
(February 28: +8th century, exact date unknown)

Basil was the disciple of St. Procopius of Decapolis, and both father and spiritual son confessed their faith and suffered for the art of the icon under the reign of Leo III the Isaurian.[50]

7. Nicetas the Confessor, Bishop of Apolonias
(March 20: +740)

Nicetas opposed the iconoclastic policy of Leo III and encouraged the faithful to continue to venerate icons. The Emperor imprisoned, tortured, and exiled him. He died in exile in 740.[51]

8. Hilarion the Younger, Hegumen and Confessor
(March 28: +754)

Hilarion was the hegumen of the Monastery of Pelecete in Bithynia during the first period of iconoclasm. His resistance to the Emperor Constantine V's policy only brought persecution down on his head. He died around 754.[52]

9. Stephen the Younger, Monk and Martyr
(November 28: +766)

Stephen became the head of the iconodules in the battle against iconoclasm during the reign of the Emperor Constantine V. As hegumen of the Monastery of Mount St. Auxentius, near Nicomedia, he received many monks that were being persecuted by the Emperor. Stephen was summoned to Constantinople to approve the decisions of the iconoclastic council of Hieria in 754, but he of course refused to comply. Even though he was tracked down, captured, tortured, exiled, and finally imprisoned in Constantinople because of his resistance, this defender of the orthodoxy of the icon never gave in to the pressure to conform. An iconoclastic crowd, which the soldiers had riled up, pulled Stephen from his prison and killed him on November 28, 766, at the age of 53.[53]

10. The Companions of Stephen the Younger
(November 28: +766)[54]

Andrew, a monk of Blachernes and a companion of St. Stephen the Younger, was dragged on the ground and died from these wounds because he continued to venerate the holy icons.

Anne was accused of infamous acts and beaten to death for having dared to support Stephen in his struggle against the iconoclasts.

John, Basil, Stephen, and a great number of other

martyrs and confessors suffered with St. Stephen the Younger because they came to the defense of the holy icons.

11. Thirty-eight Martyred Monks (November 28: +766)

Thirty-eight venerable monks fought according to the rules of combat
and were shut up in an Ephesian prison, dying from suffocation.
We the faithful, with our whole hearts, call them blessed.[55]

These nameless martyrs are mentioned in the office sung for St. Stephen the Younger on November 28. See below on the notice for St. Theosterict the Confessor, March 17, where we hear about the martyrdom of thirty-eight monks, perhaps the same ones.

12. Paul the Martyr (March 17: +766)

Paul was burned alive because of his faithfulness to the veneration of icons:
Baked in the fire like bread,
and cruelly suspended by your feet,
you were burned as a holocaust, O venerable Paul,
but our God, receiving your sacrifice,
judged you worthy of the company of the martyrs.[56]

13. Andrew the Martyr, Monk (October 17: +767)

During the reign of Constantine V Copronymus, Andrew heard rumors of the persecution against those who venerated icons, and so he left Crete to go to Constantinople to bear witness to his faith in icons. Andrew reproached the Emperor for his error and his cruelty. Not being able to stomach such audacity, Constantine had him arrested and tortured. Andrew died of his wounds in 767; his body was thrown into a pit, called Crisis, reserved for criminals. Later on, he was buried in a holy place.[57]

14. Stephen the Confessor, Bishop of Surozha in the Crimea
(December 15: +787)

Stephen came into conflict with Leo III the Isaurian over the veneration of icons and was exiled. After the death of Leo, he returned to his home and once again became the target of persecution by the iconoclasts. He died in 787.[58]

15. Theophilus the Confessor
(October 10: +8th century, exact date unknown)

Theophilus was a monk during the first iconoclastic period. When Leo III began the persecution of the Orthodox, Theophilus' firmness kept the Emperor's policy from being a success. Leo called Theophilus to the palace, but faced with the saint's assurance, the Emperor could do nothing. Flogged, then sent to Nicaea for trial, Theophilus defended icons so brilliantly that the presiding judge set him free. He went home and died in peace at an unknown date.[59]

16. Anthusa the Hegumena (July 27: +794)

Anthusa was hegumena of the monastery in Mantinea. In order to persuade her to renounce the veneration of icons, the Emperor Constantine V Copronymus sent his agent to her with the order to leave her in peace if she accepted to give up icons. If she refused, the agent was to use torture to force her to renounce them. The soldiers tied Anthusa up, flogged her, put burning icons on her head, and burned her feet with burning coals. She did not give in an inch and was exiled. After the death of Constantine, Anthusa returned to her post as hegumena, dying in peace in 794.[60]

17. Theosterict the Confessor (March 17: +after 775)

Theosterict was the hegumen of the Monastery of Pelecete during the reign of Constantine V Copronymus,

the Emperor who persecuted the Orthodox for their veneration of icons. One Holy Thursday, one of the imperial
governors, the blood-thirsty Michael Lachanodrakon, attacked Theosterict's monastery arresting thirty-eight
monks, torturing and mutilating others. The governor cut
off Theosterict's nose and imprisoned him in Constantinople along with St. Stephen the Younger and 342 other
confessors. After the iconoclastic persecution, Theosterict
returned to his monastery, which he rebuilt with the aid of
St. Nicetas of Medikion, and died in peace.[61]

B. The Second Period of Iconoclasm: 813-842

1. Plato the Studite, Confessor (April 4: +814)

Plato was the uncle of St. Theodore the Studite and
lived during the first iconoclastic period. He defended
the art of the icon and was a true confessor. His suffering,
however, was due not to his defense of icons but to other
causes.[62]

2. Thaddeus the Confessor (December 29: +around 815)

Thaddeus, a monk and disciple of St. Theodore the
Studite, was arrested by the police of Leo V the Armenian, the new iconoclastic Emperor who tried to force
the saint to renounce icons. When Thaddeus refused, the
Emperor had him flogged with 130 lashes; Thaddeus
died two days later.[63]

3. Theophanes the Confessor (March 12: +817)

Born in Constantinople in 759, Theophanes lived a
monastic life and excelled in all the virtues. Attending the
7th Ecumenical Council in 787, he impressed the Fathers
by his knowledge of the Church's Tradition. In 813, Leo
V the Armenian began once again to persecute the
iconodules and tried to convince Theophanes to abandon the veneration of icons. The Emperor imprisoned

him, but he did not give in. Theophanes was finally exiled to Samothrace and died in 817.[64]

4. Emilian the Confessor, Bishop of Cyzicus
(August 8: +813)

Emilian confessed the orthodoxy of icons at the beginning of the second iconoclastic period. Having refused to obey the orders of the Emperor, Leo V the Armenian, the bishop of Cyzicus was tortured and exiled. He died in 813 as a result of his wounds.[65]

5. John, Disciple of Gregory of Decapolis
(April 18: +820)

Along with his master, Gregory of Decapolis, John fought against the iconoclasm of Leo III the Isaurian. He died in peace in 820 and was buried beside his friend, Joseph the Hymnographer.[66]

6. George the Confessor, Bishop of Mytilene
(April 7: +821)

Having become at a young age the bishop of the island of Mytilene, George went to Constantinople to seek aid in settling a conflict with someone on Mytilene. There the Patriarch Nicephorus persuaded him to stay and help him. Both men fought Leo V the Armenian when he began to persecute the iconodules. George was arrested, beaten, and exiled; he died in 821.[67]

7. Peter and Paul the Confessors, Bishops of Nicaea
(September 10: +823)

All that we know about Peter is that he defended icons and that he died in peace in 823. Paul is not mentioned in the synaxarion, but his name is associated with Peter's in two calendars in the Russian tradition.[68]

8. Nicetas the Confessor of Medikion (April 3: +824)

Nicetas was the hegumen of the Medikion Monastery on Mount Olympus in Bithynia. When the Emperor Leo V the Armenian called all the important hegumens to Constantinople in 815 to obtain their support of his new iconoclastic policy, Nicetas replied that iconoclasm was nothing other than a refusal of the Incarnation itself. For his audacity, Nicetas was thrown into prison and tortured. Under the weight of his suffering, Nicetas and some other confessors accepted the communion of the new iconoclastic Patriarch who had replaced his orthodox predecessor, St. Nicephorus. Nicetas was sick with remorse at having accepted to be in communion with heretics and publicly repented. Again arrested, persecuted, and imprisoned, Nicetas erased his former sin through his suffering. After the death of Leo V in 820, Nicetas the Confessor took up residence near Constantinople where he died, exhausted, in 824.[69]

9. John the Psichaita, Confessor (May 7: +825)

The Greek synaxaria celebrate John on May 7 while the Russian calendars put him on May 26. John was the administrator of his monastery and succeeded his brother as hegumen around 813. Called before the iconoclastic Patriarch, Theodore Cassiteras, John confessed the orthodoxy of icon veneration and was exiled. He went back to his monastery during the lull declared by the Emperor Michael II. John died in 825.[70]

10. Athanasius the Confessor (February 22: +826)

Athanasius was the hegumen of the Sts. Peter and Paul Monastery when Leo V the Armenian renewed the persecution of those who venerated icons. With other hegumens and St. Theodore the Studite, Athanasius signed two letters to Pope Pascal I. Persecuted unceasingly by the iconoclastic emperors, Athanasius stood firm in the faith. He died suddenly in 826.[71]

11. Michael the Confessor, Metropolitan of Synnada
(May 23: +826)

Patriarch Tarasius named the monk Michael bishop of Synnada in 784. The new Bishop was thus able to participate in the 7th Ecumenical Council of Nicaea in 787. He undertook several diplomatic missions to the Arabs, Rome, and Charlemagne. Leo V the Armenian, rekindling iconoclasm in 815, demanded the support of Michael and all the Church. Since he resisted the will of the Emperor, Michael suffered imprisonment, exile, and persecution. The Emperor Michael II the Stammerer, still iconoclast but less of a persecutor, allowed the Metropolitan to return to his diocese. Michael died in the presence of Theodore the Studite in 826.[72]

12. Paul the Confessor, Bishop of Plusias
(March 8: +around 838)

Paul opposed the destruction of icons in his churches by those who preferred the images of animals, plants, and landscapes. His preaching against the iconoclasts won him exile near Mt. Olympus, a region where there was a large number of holy confessors. He died in peace between 833 and 843.[73]

13. Nicetas the Confessor (October 13: +around 838)

Nicetas had entered the service of the Empress Irene but served subsequent emperors until 811 when Michael I Rangabe allowed him to become a monk. During the iconoclastic persecutions under Leo V and Theophilus, Nicetas remained faithful to Orthodoxy and refused communion with Antonios, the iconoclastic Patriarch. Exile and wandering naturally followed. His disciples and he finally found a safe, isolated place where they built a church. Nicetas lived there in peace until he was 75. He died in 838.[74]

14. Theophylact the Confessor, Bishop of Nicomedia
(March 8: +840)

Theophylact was a civil servant who worked for the future Patriarch Tarasius, then became a monk in the monastery founded by Tarasius, and finally accepted to become Bishop of Nicomedia at the request of Tarasius. He was a devoted pastor of the Church of Nicomedia until the day when Leo V the Armenian opened the second iconoclastic period. In 815, Patriarch Theophylact and other iconodule bishops gathered together in Constantinople to convince the Emperor of his error. Exasperated, Leo exiled the bishops all over the Empire. Theophylact went to Strobilos where he spent 30 years in prison. It was there that he wrote many letters to the Orthodox encouraging them to resist the heresy. He died in 840.[75]

15. Theodore the Branded (December 27: +840)

Born in Jerusalem in 775, Theodore received his education in St. Sabbas Monastery. His brother Theophanes and he became spiritual sons of St. Michael the Syncellos and followed him on his mission to Rome and Constantinople. Leo V the Armenian imprisoned the two brothers in a fortress until the reign of Michael II who, being less ferocious than his predecessor, let them free and to live in peace at St. Michael's Monastery in Sosthenion. The Emperor Theophilus arrested them again in 834 and demanded that they condemn the veneration of icons. They resisted, and the Emperor once more threw them into prison. Two years later, Theodore and Theophanes were branded on the forehead and exiled to Bithynia because they had the audacity to calmly answer the Emperor's arguments against icons. In Bithynia, Theodore died as a result of his many years of suffering.[76]

16. Macarius the Confessor, Hegumen of the Pelecete Monastery (April 1: +840)

Macarius was born at Constantinople around 750 and became a monk, then hegumen, of the Pelecete Monastery near Mount Olympus in Bithynia. He was known, even to the Empress Irene, for his healing power. Patriarch Tarasius ordained him a priest. To win him over to iconoclasm, Leo V the Armenian offered Macarius honors and riches, but without any effect. Naturally, the saint was arrested and sent into exile. During the lull of Michael II's reign, Macarius recovered some of the freedom that he would soon lose under Theophilus, a hardened iconoclast. Once again, the Emperor tried seduction, but without any results. Macarius found himself once more in prison where he preached Orthodoxy to the Paulician heretics and to other iconoclastic prisoners. Theophilus, being very irritated by Macarius' action, exiled him once more. The Confessor died in 840 surrounded by the many monks who had followed him into exile.[77]

17. Naucratius the Studite (April 18: +844)

Naucratius was a disciple and successor of Theodore the Studite at the Studion Monastery. Under Leo V the Armenian, he was imprisoned and tortured for upholding the veneration of icons. He then directed the Studion during Theophilus' persecution. As a reward, Naucratius was present at the final victory over iconoclasm in 843; he died in 848.[78]

18. Theophanes the Branded, Hymnographer (October 11: +845)

Theophanes was born in Palestine, like his brother Theodore the Branded, in 778, and followed the same path as his brother until the latter's death in 840. After the Emperor Theophilus died in 842, Theophanes was elected metropolitan of Nicaea where he died in peace in 845.[79]

19. Michael the Syncellos, Confessor (December 18: +846)

After living as a monk in Jerusalem, Michael spent some time in Constantinople in 813 at the time when the Emperor Leo V the Armenian and the Patriarch Theodotus renewed iconoclasm for the second time. He did not hesitate to denounce the heresy, was arrested, and put in prison until 820 when the new Emperor, Michael II, also iconoclast but less of a persecutor, exiled him to a monastery in Bithynia. In 834, after the death of Michael II, the iconoclastic Emperor Theophilus put Michael in prison again where he became hunchback and nearly blind. Freed by the iconodule Empress, Theodora, Michael was acclaimed a hero and confessor of Orthodoxy because of his sufferings. He died at 85 in 846.[80]

20. Methodius the Patriarch of Constantinople, Confessor (June 14: +847)

Just before 811, Methodius entered the Chenolakkos Monastery in Bithynia where he became known for his calligraphy, among other things. The Patriarch Nicephorus persuaded him to join his clergy as an archdeacon and named him hegumen of his monastery. When Leo V the Armenian unleashed a new round of iconoclasm in 815, Methodius left his monastery in 817 and went to Rome looking for support for Orthodoxy. Even though he returned to Constantinople in 820 with documents written in support of Orthodoxy by Pope Pascal I, Methodius was not able to convince the new Emperor, Michael II the Stammerer, to abandon iconoclasm. He was, of course, exiled, imprisoned, and persecuted until the death of the last iconoclastic Emperor, Theophilus, in 842. At the council of 843 where the Empress Theodora had the heretical Patriarch deposed, Methodius was elected Patriarch. With the other confessors of the icon, he participated in the final victory of iconodulia over iconoclasm. He died in peace in 847.[81]

A great number of martyrs and confessors bore witness to the orthodoxy of the icon in the second iconoclastic period, but since they were exiled all over the Empire, we do not know the exact dates of their deaths. We therefore simply indicate "+before 850."

21. Clement the Hymnographer, Confessor
(April 30: +before 850)

Clement was a monk of the Studion Monastery and the "beloved son" of Theodore the Studite. He confessed the orthodoxy of icon veneration during the second iconoclastic period. He wrote hymns to the Mother of God and to the saints, dying at an unknown date.[82]

22. Euschemon the Confessor, Bishop of Lampsacus
(March 14: +before 850)

Along with St. Theodore the Studite, Euschemon vigorously defended icons against the iconoclastic Emperor Theophilus. For this, he was imprisoned and exiled. He died at an unknown date.[83]

23. James the Confessor, Bishop (March 21: +before 850)

James was the spiritual son of St. Theodore the Studite, and after his episcopal consecration, he stood up against the iconoclasts. He was persecuted and exiled, dying during the first half of the 9th century.[84]

24. Eustathius the Confessor, Bishop of Kios in Bithynia
(March 29: +before 850)

Eustathius bore witness to icons during the second iconoclastic period. For his defense of icons, he was persecuted, exiled, and tortured. He died in exile at an unknown date.

25. Basil the Confessor, Bishop of Parion
(April 11: +before 850)

Between 813 and 820, Basil refused to accept the

iconoclastic policy of Leo V. He therefore spent his life in exile, wandering here and there until he died at an unknown date.[86]

26. Stephen the Confessor, Hegumen of Triglia
March 26: +before 850

Leo V the Armenian tried to force Stephen to sign an iconoclastic statement when the Emperor started to persecute those who venerated icons. The Bishop refused, was tortured, and died in exile.[87]

27. Cosmas the Confessor, Bishop of Chalcedon
(April 18: +before 850)

Cosmas and his friend Auxentius bore witness to Orthodoxy and suffered for their veneration of icons during the second period of iconoclasm.[88]

28. George the Confessor, Bishop of Antioch in Pisidia
(Date of Death Uncertain)

Having been called to Constantinople to subscribe to iconoclasm, George refused; as a result, he was exiled and persecuted.[89]

29. Sergius, Irene, and Their Children, Confessors
(May 13: +before 850)

Two synaxaria of the Greek tradition call the head of this family *Sergius,* and two calendars of the Russian tradition call him *George.* The four sources agree, however, about the date. Because of the witness of the father (Sergius/George) in favor of icons during the persecution of Theophilus around 835, all the members of the family suffered exile and persecution.[90]

30. Nicetas, Bishop of Chalcedon; Ignatius, and Nicetas,
Confessors (May 28: +before 850)

We have very little information about these three men except that they were of the same family and confessed the orthodoxy of icon veneration during the second iconoclastic period.[91]

31. Nicholas the Studite, Confessor (February 4: +868)

Nicholas was the nephew of St. Theodore the Studite and the faithful spiritual son of his uncle in the Studion Monastery. When Leo V the Armenian rekindled the persecution of the Orthodox in 815 and up until the death of St. Theodore in 826, Nicholas shared with his uncle persecution, torture, exile, and imprisonment because of their firmness in Orthodoxy. After the death of Theodore, Nicholas had to endure alone the horrors of persecution until the final victory over iconoclasm in 843. Then, everyone recognized him as a confessor of the faith. Nicholas continued his monastic life until his death in 868 at the age of 75.[92]

V. The Holy Defenders and Theologians of the Icon

1. Saint Gregory II, Pope of Rome (February 11: +731)

Gregory headed the Roman Church when Leo III the Isaurian opened his iconoclastic campaign in 726. The Emperor had written to the Pope hoping to convince him to support his new policy. In two answers to the Emperor, the Pope refuted Leo's arguments including his claim to be both "Emperor and priest." Gregory supported all the Orthodox, including Germanus the Patriarch of Constantinople, against the harassment and persecution carried out by the iconoclasts.

2. Saint John of Damascus, Monk and Iconologist (December 4: +780)

John was born in Damascus, the capital of Syria, around 680. His father, Sergius Mansur, worked as a civil servant for Abdul-Malik, the Muslim Caliph. Due to his talent and intelligence, John was destined to follow in his father's footsteps, after the latter's death, and to serve the sovereign. John did serve the Caliph, for a time, but resigned and went to the Saint Sabbas Monastery near Jerusalem. Around 730, when the Emperor Leo III began to destroy icons in the Byzantine Empire, John found himself in a very secure place from which to denounce the new imperial policy. Since he was under the jurisdiction of another monarch, he had no fear of reprisals. He wrote three treatises against iconoclasm: *On the Divine Images.*[94] These formed the first thought-out response to the attacks of those who considered icons to be idols. His presentation of the theology of the icon has become classic. Even during his life, John of Damascus was the champion of the iconodules and the great adversary of the iconoclasts. The iconoclastic council of Hieria in 754 as well as the 7th Ecumenical Council of Nicaea in 787 quoted his works. John spent the rest of his life in the monastery where he continued to write in defense of Orthodoxy and to instruct his fellow monks. He died as a very old man around 780.[95]

3. Saint Tarasius, Patriarch of Constantinople
(February 25: +806)

Tarasius grew up in a noble family of Constantinople, and when the Emperor Leo IV died in 780, he assumed the post of prime minister for the Empress Irene who became regent during the minority of her son Constantine VI. Just having come out of the first iconoclastic period, the Church of Constantinople needed a strong hand to reestablish Orthodoxy. The old Patriarch Paul was not the man for the job. Irene chose rather Tarasius to assure the direction of the Church. Tarasius finally accepted after requiring the convocation of an ecumenical council to deal once and for all with the question of icon veneration. The iconoclasts sabotaged the first convocation of the council in August 786; the second attempt succeeded, and the 7th Ecumenical Council opened on September 24, 787, in Nicaea. By his gentle spirit, the Patriarch tried to reconcile the moderate iconoclasts to Orthodoxy by setting aside the sanctions that he judged too severe; many wanted to treat the iconoclasts very harshly. This irenic policy only won for him the opposition of other confessors like Plato and Theodore the Studite who wanted to show no mercy to the repentant heretics. In this case, however, the Church accepted Tarasius' conciliatory policy. After the victory over the iconoclasts at the Second Council of Nicaea, Patriarch Tarasius guided the Byzantine Church during another 19 years. He died in 806 as a result of a sickness from which he had suffered many years.[96]

4. The Fathers of the 7th Ecumenical Council of Nicaea (The Sunday between October 11-17: 787)

This council was held from September 24 through October 13, 787, at which 350 bishops, some 135 hegumens, and 17 repentant iconoclastic bishops gathered to defeat the iconoclastic heresy. Patriarch Tarasius of Constantinople presided in the presence of representatives from Rome, Antioch, and Jerusalem. The council proclaimed that the making of icons and their veneration are in agreement with the Gospel. The Fathers clearly distinguished between an idol and an icon, on the one hand, and the worship given to God and the veneration offered to persons and objects worthy of respect, on the other.[97]

5. Saint Nicephorus the Confessor, Patriarch of Constantinople (June 2: +828)

Nicephorus was born around 758 in Constantinople into a bourgeois family, and all his intellectual education was intended to prepare him for the civil service of the Empire. In fact, he became a secretary at the court of Constantine V Copronymus. He kept his post and increased his influence during the regency of the Empress Irene and the patriarchate of Tarasius. He participated actively in the debates about the icon at the Council of Nicaea II in 787. After the council, Nicephorus retired to Propontis where he lived in tranquillity. When he returned to Constantinople, Patriarch Tarasius asked him to administer an orphanage, and he accepted. In 806, Tarasius died, and the Emperor Nicephorus I promoted the secretary Nicephorus to the patriarchal throne, not without provoking opposition among the Studite monks because of Nicephorus' rapid and unusual advancement. Leo V succeeded to the imperial throne in 813 and started the second iconoclastic period. The Patriarch refused to bow to the Emperor's will and was exiled in 815. He spent the rest of his life in exile and produced a great number of texts against the iconoclasts, among which we have *Discourses Against the Iconoclasts* written between 818 and 820. After John of Damascus, Nicephorus is the second theological Father of the icon. He died in 828.[98]

6. Saint Theodore the Studite, Monk and Confessor
(November 11: +826)

Born in 759 in Constantinople, Theodore became a monk under his uncle Plato's influence; he progressed rapidly in the esteem of Plato and his fellow monks. He was named hegumen of the Saccudion Monastery and later of the Studion Monastery in Constantinople. There Theodore inaugurated a reform of the monastic life and opposed all interference of the Emperor in the affairs of the Church. It is not surprising, therefore, that Theodore obstinately refused to submit to the Emperor's will. Naturally, Leo V exiled and persecuted him, but by his letters and writings, Theodore encouraged the orthodox resistance. In one of his treatises, *On the Holy Images,* he became a theological defender of the icon, the third Father after John of Damascus and Patriarch Nicephorus to express in words and concepts the mind of the Church on this question. Because of the rigor of his ascetical life, his numerous exiles, and his struggle for the independence of the Church in relation to the Emperor, Theodore the Studite exhausted all his human strength, and at the age of 67, in 826, he fell asleep in the Lord.[99]

7. Saint Theodora the Empress (February 11: 867)

Theodora was the wife of Theophilus, the last iconoclastic Emperor, who outdid everyone else in his cruelty: he ferociously persecuted the iconodules. Despite the fact that her husband opposed the veneration of icons, Theodora continued to do so in private. When Theophilus died in 843, the Empress assumed the regency in the name of her young son, Michael III. With the help of the new Patriarch, Methodius the Confessor, she convoked a council to reestablish the veneration of icons in the churches, anathematize the heretics, confirm Nicaea II as the 7th Ecumenical Council, and rehabilitate all the confessors of the second iconoclastic period. This council took place in Constantinople in 843 and established the feast of the Triumph of Orthodoxy for the first Sunday of Great Lent. In 850, due to the intrigues at court, Theodora was forced to retire to a monastery where she lived until her death in 867.[100]

VI. Masters of the Icon[101]

1. Theophanes the Greek
(end of 14th century, beginning of the 15th century)

See the Annex for the opinion that Epiphanius the Wise had about Theophanes the Greek.[102]

Theophanes arrived in Moscow around 1395 and was greatly admired by Russian painters. He had the reputation of a great painter and a fine theologian. Epiphanius the Wise said of Theophanes that he "understood the faraway and the spiritual with his mind, for he perceived spiritual beauty through his enlightened bodily eyes."[103] The Chronicles often speak of him:

In the same year [1378] was painted the church of Our Lord Jesus Christ on Iljina Street at the behest of the noble and God-loving bojar Vasiliy Danilovich and the dwellers of the street. It was the Greek master Theophanes who painted it at the time of the Grand Prince Dimitry Ivanovich and Lexij, archbishop of Novgorod the Great and Pskov.[104]

In the same year [1395], on the 4th of June, a Thursday, at the time of mass, the new stone church of the Nativity of the holy Mother of God at Moscow began to be painted. The masters were the icon-painter Theophanes, who was a Greek philosopher, as well as Semen Chernyj and their pupils.[105]

In the same year [1399] was painted the stone church of St. Michael at Moscow by the Greek icon-painter Theophanes, who was the master, and by his pupils.[106]

It is generally accepted that Theophanes was Andrei Rublev's teacher, or at least one of them. The Chronicle gives this impression:

> In the spring of that year [1405] the stone church of the holy Annunciation in the Grand Prince's palace — not the one that is standing now — began to be painted. The masters were the Greek icon-painter Theophanes, the elder monk Prokhor from Gorodets, and the monk Andrej Rublev. They finished in the same year.[107]

2. Manuel Panselinos, George Kaliergis, Michael and Eutychios Astrapas of Thessalonica (end of the 13th century, beginning of the 14th century)

These very active fresco painters represent the Thessalonica school; they manifested the dynamism of the Palaeologan Renaissance. We know very little about Panselinos, but tradition says that he painted frescoes in the Protaton Church of Mount Athos around the beginning of the 14th century. The only written confirmation of this tradition is found in the work of Dionysius of Fourna, written around 1730:

… the master of Thessalonica, Manuel Panselinos, who was compared with the brilliance of the moon; this painter having worked on the Holy Mountain of Athos, painting holy icons and beautiful churches, shone in his profession of painting so that this brilliance exceeded that of the moon, and he obscured with his miraculous art all painters, both ancient and modern, as is shown most clearly by the walls and panels that were painted with images by him… .[108]

Panselinos was a master of the Macedonian school, a branch of the Athonite school of painting, alongside that of Crete. His frescoes on Mount Athos reflect a deep spirituality. We must not forget that at the time of Panselinos, the 14th century, the Church of Constantinople was living its final glory, the Palaeologan Renaissance, and that Mount Athos was agitated by the Hesychastic controversies between St. Gregory Palamas and Barlaam of Calabria. The Byzantine Church was debating the place of the uncreated Light in the vision of God. It is therefore normal to note that an artist of the time would have been sensitive to the subject of light in both spirituality and painting. This is the same marriage between the mystical light and artistic light that Russians painters will celebrate some centuries later.[109]

3. Daniel Chorny, Friend and Companion of Andrei Rublev (1365-1430)

Daniel was a monk of the Spasso-Andronikof Monastery where he met Andrei Rublev who himself had just arrived. Andrei took Daniel as his teacher. They became very good friends and worked together nearly all their lives. Andrei called him his "friend and companion in fasting." Around 1408, Daniel, Andrei Rublev, and other artists painted the Dormition Cathedral in Vladimir. Since they were such good friends and worked so closely together, it is nearly impossible to separate the lives of Daniel and Andrei; the historical documents nearly always speak about them together. According to the witness of St. Joseph of Volokolamsk, who was the first to write about their legendary friendship, only death could separate them, physically but not spiritually. Andrei died first, but Daniel had a vision at the end of his life and saw his friend in heaven: "Daniel then fell ill, and during his last moments, he saw his companion Andrei in a great and glorious light. Andrei called Daniel to come join him in eternal and infinite happiness."[110] It is not out of place to wonder why the Russian Church did not also glorify Daniel at the canonization of Andrei Rublev in 1988. We have found two statements about "saint" Daniel. One is found in the notice for St. Nikon of Radonezh: "In 1422, the relics of St. Serge were transported ... to the new church decorated with admirable frescoes painted by Sts. Daniel the Black [Chorny] and Andrei Rublev."[111] The other comes from Leonid Ouspensky: during "the XIVth and the XVth centuries ... St. Andrew (Rublev) ... worked with his friend and teacher, St. Daniel (the Black)."[112] Do these authors have access to little known sources, or are they expressing their personal opinion?[113] See the Annex, #13.

4. Dionysius of Moscow (1445?-1505?)

Dionysius was born around 1445, a little after the death of Andrei Rublev. He, along with his two sons, and his group of artists, for whom he was the master painter, extended the iconographic tradition already developed by Rublev and his companions. Around 1467, Dionysius was part of the fresco painters' cooperative (*artel*), directed by Mitrophanes. The frescoes painted by Dionysius in the Church of the Nativity in a monastery near Moscow so impressed Tsar Ivan III that he invited Dionysius to come work in Moscow. Due to his great reputation, Dionysius received orders from everywhere. In 1481, he and the members of his cooperative were asked to paint the Dormition Cathedral in the Moscow Kremlin. Around 1483, Dionysius painted the Church of Our Savior in front of the Kremlin. After the fire of 1547, which had destroyed a large part of Moscow, the chronicle says that the painting of this church "…was a marvel, the work of Dionysius the icon-painter… ."[114] Between 1484 and 1486, again near Moscow, Dionysius and his artists decorated the Monastery of St. Joseph of Volokolamsk. In the *Life of Joseph Volotsky*, the author speaks of these decorations: "Its [the monastery's] decoration was done by the most cunning [most sophisticated and skillful] painters in the Russian land… ."[115] This is an obvious reference to Dionysius and his companions. The last work that we know about from historical documents is dated 1502-1503 when Dionysius and his sons worked at the Monastery of the Nativity of the Virgin near Vologda. Dionysius died between 1503 and 1508. The famous treatise *Message to an Iconographer* which we suppose was written by St. Joseph of Volokolamsk for Dionysius, reflects the hesychastic vision that is the theoretical background of all of Dionysius' work. The *Message* and the works of art produced by Dionysius and his companions are identical in content: "…an art characterized by the same perfect fusion of dogmatic content, inner prayer, and artistic creation."[116] It is interesting to note that Dionysius was married. The vocation of an iconographer is not therefore limited to monks. Any Orthodox Christian, man or woman, can open himself to the experience of the prayer of the heart and can, if he has sufficient talent, express this deep experience by painting icons.[117]

5. Theophanes of Crete (1500?-1559)

Theophanes is the greatest painter of what the specialists call the Cretan school. Scholarly opinion is, however, divided on the question of the origin, and even the existence, of the Cretan "school," but we think that this school has its roots in the paintings done in Crete during the 14th century. In any case, the Cretan style is not limited to the island because the artists who imitated it spread it all over the Orthodox world. History knows Theophanes as a monk, but he had two sons who were also painters. He was therefore married. Perhaps his wife died when he was young, and then in later life he became a monk.[118]

6. Dionysius of Fourna (1670?-1746)

Dionysius was a Greek iconographer, a priest-monk, born around 1670 in Fourna in Agrapha, central Greece. He went to Mount Athos many times and there learned the art of painting. Later in his own region, around 1743, he established a monastery that was also a school for training iconographers. Nonetheless, he is not known for his works, even though certain ones still exist today, but mainly for his *Painter's Manual* (*Hermeneia*) which he wrote probably between 1730 and 1734. This manual is for iconographers, contains verbal descriptions of the saints and feasts, and is intended to help iconographers in their work. Dionysius died around 1746.[119]

7. Simon Ushakov (1626-1686)

Ushakov was, perhaps, the greatest Russian painter of the 17th century. From 1664 to his death in 1686, he directed the tsar's icon studio; he was called "the tsar's chief iconographer." Under his inspiration, new elements were introduced into the art of the icon: natural likeness, perspective, oil painting, and other techniques and styles from the West. He also wrote a treatise, *Discourse to the One Who Has Zeal for the Painting of Icons*, in which he defended his ideas on art. Simon Ushakov is still controversial today. The question is just how to evaluate his work. Did he save, renew, even modernize, Russian sacred art by integrating the ideals and techniques of Western painting into traditional iconography? Or did he open the door to influences foreign to the spirit of the icon, thus provoking a drift away from the iconographic tradition, even an abandoning of it? Opinions continue to differ about the evaluation of Ushakov and his work. One thing is certain, however, and all the experts agree: Ushakov changed the orientation of Russian sacred art by introducing new elements mainly borrowed from Western Europe. If we take the works of the classical period, that is, of Rublev, Theophanes the Greek, Dionysius, etc., as the authentic expression in art of the Orthodox theological vision — this is our point of view — then it is difficult to remain indifferent to the changes introduced by Ushakov and his disciples. However, everyone does not share this opinion. It is nonetheless regrettable that the Russian society of the 17th century was not able to create a "two-storied" art: one level being a Western European, "secularized" painting fully inspired by the principles and vision of contemporary Western painters and the other being the icon inspired by the iconographic and canonical tradition of the past. Ushakov remains nonetheless an unavoidable figure in the long history of the icon.[120]

8. Joseph Vladimirov (middle of the 17th century)

Joseph Vladimirov was a painter and fellow worker with Simon Ushakov; he too promoted the new ideas and techniques introduced during the 17th century. He wrote a *Letter of a Certain Iconographer Joseph to the Iconographer of the Tsar, the Wise Simon Theodorovich* in which he expounded his ideas and complained about the abuses rampant in his time. What we have said about Ushakov concerning the ambiguity of the changes brought about in traditional iconography is equally true for Vladimirov.[121]

9. Leonid Ouspensky, Iconographer and Iconologist (1902-1987)

It is difficult not to underline the importance of this

painter and thinker for the renaissance of the canonical icon in the 20th century. By his writings and his works, he preached one simple idea: icons are the visible representation, in forms and colors, of the theological vision of the Orthodox Church's ecclesial tradition. The rediscovery and the spread of this vision, darkened during such a long period, was the main vocation of his life. Ouspensky worked in three areas: history, theology, and painting. He studied and taught the long history of Christian art in general and the icon in particular. He explained the meaning, that is, the theological vision behind the historical development and production of the icon. And finally, he made the vision visible by painting it in his works. By mobilizing all his talents, so admirably expressed in *The Theology of the Icon* and in other writings, Leonid Ouspensky put a new luster on an art that had been darkened by an estrangement from its own sources.[122]

10. Photios Kontoglou, Iconographer and Iconologist (1895-1965)

Photios Kontoglou is in the Greek world what Ouspensky is in the Russian. Both men actively participated in the renewal of the icon that had begun at the beginning of the 20th century. Kontoglou, less known to Westerners than Ouspensky, was a painter and author. He defended the canonical icon in words and images. Kontoglou was born in Kydoniai (Aivali), presently in Turkey, in 1895. He studied painting in Paris but moved to Athens in 1922 where he discovered the grandeur of the canonical tradition of the icon. Kontoglou and his artists painted many churches in Greece, and his icons are known all over the world. His literary activity began in 1919. In his writings, which include a Greek translation of one of Ouspensky's writings, *The Icon: Some Words on Its Dogmatic Meaning* (1948), he defended the integrity of Byzantine iconography as an expression of the theological vision of the Orthodox faith. In his preface to *The Icon* ..., Kontoglou bore witness to the spiritual communion that existed between the two great promoters of authentic iconography in the 20th century.

The love that unites Christians does not come from their will ... but it is Christ that unites them ... .It is such a love that unites us, my very dear brother in Christ, Leonid Ouspensky, and me. I have never seen him with my physical eyes, and he has never seen me either..., but the one has loved the other with a new heart given by the Lord himself ... .From among the many, many men so busy running after the vanities of this world, I have heard his voice, and I understand, for he speaks a new language.[123]

11. Gregory (George) Kroug (1908-1969)

George Kroug was born in Saint-Petersburg into a religiously mixed family: his father was Swedish and Lutheran, his mother Russian and Orthodox; he grew up in the Protestant faith. Between 1921 and 1931, George studied graphic art and music. In 1931, at the age of 23, when he had just arrived in Paris, he met Leonid Ouspensky in a group of Russian artists. The two painters became intimate friends. There, in France, George pursued his life as an artist. Around the end of the 1920's, he discovered Orthodoxy and joined the Brotherhood of St. Photius, along with Ouspensky. In 1933, George began to paint the iconostasis of a Russian church in Paris, rue Pétel. He studied iconography, painted icons, and entered the monastic life in 1948. Taking the name of Gregory, George Kroug was tonsured a monk and lived for a time with his spiritual father, Archimandrite Sergius; later on, however, he moved to the skete of the Holy Spirit at Mesnil-Saint-Denis. There he gave himself over to painting icons. During the last years of his life, Fr. Gregory was sick but refused all medical help. In 1968, his health declined rapidly. He died in his skete on June 12,

1969. Father Gregory was a theologian in the Orthodox meaning of the word: he was a man profoundly steeped in prayer, and he lived the mystical vision of the faith. As an artist, he knew how to express that vision in his icons.[124]

VII. Little Known Iconographers

1. Methodius the Iconographer (864)

The exact identity of Methodius is unknown, but he played a major role in the conversion of Bulgaria to Christianity. Thanks to an icon painted by him, King Boris of the Bulgarians accepted baptism in 864. The Byzantine chronicler, John Scylitzes, 11th century, tells the following story:

> When Boris built a new home, he ordered one of the monks of Greek origin, Methodius by name and a painter by craft, to decorate the whole building with images. But prompted by some divine suggestion, he did not expressly indicate what precisely and which animals the artist was to depict, but ordered him to paint only such as he wished, provided his paintings were terrible and would arouse amazement and awe in the viewers. The monk, knowing nothing more terrible than the Second Coming of Christ, painted that scene there. The Prince, seeing the multitudes of the crowned righteous on the one side, and the multitudes of punished sinners on the other, and hearing the painter explain the meaning of the painting, immediately renounced his former faith.[125]

The chronicler mentions that Boris received baptism that very evening. There is a certain controversy about the identity of this Methodius. Some indications seem to establish a link between Methodius the iconographer and St. Methodius the Evangelizer of the Slavs. This identity is, however, not firmly established, and the mystery remains.[126]

2. Jovan of Ochrid (1266-1267)

Between 1266 and 1267, Jovan the iconographer painted an icon of St. George for a deacon, also named Jovan, who was attached to the Archbishop of Ochrid[127] On an inscription, Jovan wrote his name.

3. Theodore of Cythera (13th century)

Theodore painted frescoes on the island of Cythera. His style is similar to what we find on Crete at the same period.[128] He is known only because he wrote his name on one of the frescoes.

4. Alexis Petrov, Novgorodian Iconographer (1294)

In 1294, an icon painter named Alexis Petrov painted an icon of St. Nicholas in Novgorod. On the lower edge of the icon, he wrote his name and date.[129]

5. Prokopius of Tver (1300)

Around 1280-1320, Prince Michael Yaroslavich of Tver ordered a copy of *The Chronicle of George Harmatolos,* presently in the Lenin Library. This document contains 127 miniature paintings by several artists. One of these painters had far more talent than the others and painted the images at the beginning of the book. The first image shows Christ seated on a throne; on one side is Prince Michael, and on the other is his mother Xenia. The second image shows the monk George Harmatolos writing his chronicle. The following inscription is written on one of the images: "The servant of the Lord, Prokopius, sinner, painted this."[130]

6. Isaiah the Greek and His Companions, Iconographers in Novgorod (1338)

According to the *Chronicle of Novgorod,* on June 25, 1336, Bishop Basil of Novgorod had a stone church built; on September 21, 1337, it was finished and consecrated by Bishop Basil. Eight months later, in 1338, the *Chronicle* says the following: "The same year Bishop Basil ordered the Church of the Entrance of Our Lord Jesus Christ into Jerusalem to be painted by Isaiah a Greek, with others, on May 4, the Day of the Holy Martyr Selivian; they began to paint it the same day." The following year, 1339, we read that "the same year they finished the painting of the *Vladyka*'s Church." The iconographers, therefore, finished their work between August 13 and October 5, 1339. These are the dates the *Chronicle* gives during which "they finished the painting... ."[131]

7. Zacharias, Joseph, Nicholas, and Their Companions (1344)

In the same year [1344] two stone churches in Moscow began to be painted, that of the holy Mother of God and that of St. Michael. [The church of] the holy Mother of God was painted by Greeks, painters of the Metropolitan Theognostos, and in the same year they started they also finished. As for St. Michael's, it was painted by Russian painters, men of the Grand Prince Semen Ivanocic, and the elders and chiefs among these painters were Zacharias, Joseph, Nicholas and their companions. However, they were unable that year to paint even half of the church on account of its size.[132]

8. Goitan, Semion, and Ivan (1344)

According to the chronicles, in 1344, during the episcopate of Metropolitan Theogostos, a Greek, (1328-1353), a group of painters "of Russian origin but students of Greeks [Goitan, Semion, and Ivan]" painted the Metropolitan's church.[133]

9. John Theorianos (1350)

Theorianos was a Greek artist who worked in Ochrid. He is probably known because he wrote his name somewhere.[134]

10. Simon Chorny (1395)

According to *The Troitskaya Chronicle,* "in the same year [1395], on the 4th of June, a Thursday, at the time of mass, the new stone church of the Nativity of the holy Mother of God at Moscow began to be painted. The masters were the icon-painter Theophanes, who was a Greek philosophe r, as well as Semen Chernyj and their pupils." This Simon Chorny, was he related to Daniel Chorny, the iconographer and companion of Andrei Rublev?[135]

11. Metropolitan Jovan and His Brother Macarius (1380-1420)

Metropolitan Jovan worked to give a new birth to the tradition of monumental Serbian iconography. Fr. Macarius painted icons on wood; he was also a fresco painter in Liubostinia and in Zrze, Serbia.[136]

12. Pereplav and His Companions, Iconographers from Pskov (around 1490)

Archbishop Gennadius of Novgorod (1484-1504) criticized the iconographers of Pskov for not painting icons as did the artists of Novgorod and Moscow, that is, for not following the "new art" of the capital. The Pskovians preferred to maintain their own customs modeled on the Greeks and ancient traditions:

> And having stood up, the great icon painter Pereplav, along with other painters, declared the following: "Your Eminence, we paint these icons according to those of the ancient workshops, and we have spent our apprenticeships working with these icons which were painted according to Greek icons. But, your Eminence, there was no indication as to how to work." And so the people of Pskov listened to the icon painters rather than to the Archbishop.[137]

13. Prokhor of Gorodets (1405)

According to *The Troitskaya Chronicle,* "in the spring

of that year [1405] the stone church of the holy Annunciation in the Grand Prince's palace—not the one that is standing now—began to be painted. The masters were the Greek icon painter Theophanes, the elder monk Prokhor from Gorodets, and the monk Andrej Rublev. They finished in the same year."[138]

14. Ostania, Yakov, Mikhailo, Yokouchko, and Semion of the Exalted Word, Painter of Pskov (1547)

In 1547, a fire ravaged the buildings of the Moscow Kremlin including several churches. In order to restore these churches, Metropolitan Macarios of Moscow hired iconographers from Pskov to paint four large panels for the Annunciation Cathedral of the Kremlin. Three of these images still exist today: the *Renovation of the Temple by the Resurrection,* the *Crucifixion Surrounded by Gospel Parables,* and the *Four-part Icon* . This last image provoked quite a controversy because of its complicated and exaggerated symbolism as well as by its depiction of God the Father. Viskovaty, the Secretary of State, criticized these images as unwarranted innovations and a betrayal of the iconographic tradition. Metropolitan Macarius had Viskovaty condemned at a council in Moscow in 1553-1554.[139] The polemic surrounding the image of God the Father along with the exaggerated symbolism of these paintings exploded into open controversy in the "Viskovaty affair" and continues to provoke debate. It is interesting to note that many art historians, as well as theologians, identify this period, the middle of the 16th century, as the beginning of the degradation, of the abandonment of ancient Russian art:

> The *Four-part Icon* symbolically represents the teachings of the Church. Such a symbolism undermines the very foundations of icon painting ... .This experience signifies the beginning of the end for the icon painting of ancient Russia, an art that had existed for several centuries.[140]

According to the instincts nourished by the iconographic tradition, Viskovaty knew that this image betrayed the canons of the art of the icon, but he was condemned just the same. Other authors have subsequently defended Viskovaty, implicitly criticizing the one who was in fact the real innovator both in painting and in theological justification.[141] The irony of the whole affair is that the Russian Church recently glorified Metropolitan Macarius as a saint. Happily, we are not required, even for the saints, to accept all their opinions without critical analysis in the light of Holy Tradition. In his discussion of the image of the Trinity,[142] which shows the ambiguity of such direct representations of the Trinity, G. Kroug wisely recognizes that the question is not at all settled:

> It is probable that the question of the representation of the Trinity will once again in the future become the subject of conciliar discussion. And in the light of conciliar decisions already taken, the Church will define and establish the Orthodox iconography of the Trinity .... There is no doubt that these questions, which have not been fully studied in the light of the Church's vision, will be completely enlightened and resolved in a conciliar definition of the Church.[143]

15. Iconographers from Crete during the Venetian Period (1204-1669)[144]

a) Nicholas the Reader, 13th century: This artist finished painting the Church of St. George in Sclavopoula in western Crete around 1290.

b) John Pagomenos, +around 1347: Pagomenos worked in western Crete from 1313 to 1347. He is the best known of all the artists of Crete.

c) Daniel and Michael Veneris, Uncle and Nephew: These two artists were contemporaries of Pagomenos and also painted in western Crete.

d) George Provatopoulos, Paul Provatas, Nicholas Mstrachas, George Partzalis, Xenos Diogenes, Fr.

Anastasios, and Dracopoulos, 14th and 15th centuries: All these artists painted in western Crete.

e) George the Painter, Fr. John Moussouros, Constantine Ricos, George Pelegris, and the brothers Manual and John Phocas, 14th and 15th centuries: These artists were active in western Crete.

16. The Cretan School after the Fall of Constantinople: (1453 to the 17th century)

These artists painted in the Cretan style even though they did not all work exclusively in Crete. After the fall of Crete to the Turks in 1669, artistic activity on the island greatly diminished and finally ended altogether.[145]

a) Andrew (+1492) and Nicholas (+before 1507) Ritzos, father and son.

b) Andrew Pavias (+after 1504) and his disciple Angelos Bizamanos (+1530?).

c) Nicholas Tzafuaris (+before 1509).

d) Simon and Neophytes, sons of Theophanes the Cretan (1540-1590).

e) Michael Damaskinos of Heraclion (1560-1600).

f) George Klotzas (+1608)

g) Jeremiah Palladas, Frangias Kavertzas, Emmanuel Tzanfournaris, Angelos, Fr. John Apakas, and Emmanuel Lambardos (1600-1650).

h) Emmanuel Tzanes Bounialis (1610-1690) and Theodore Poulakis (1622-1692).

17. Fr. Timothy, Yarets, Konia, Dosithius, Paissius, and Bassianus (1480-1500)

These artists were part of the artistic cooperative of Dionysius of Moscow.[146]

18. Mitrophanes the Monk (1480-1500)

A monk in St. Simon's Monastery in Moscow, Mitrophanes directed an artists' cooperative (*artel*) in which Dionysius was a member. We can assume that

Mitrophanes was therefore Dionysius' teacher. Metrophanes' fresco painters, including Dionysius, painted the Nativity Cathedral in the Monastery of Paphnutius-Borovsk built in 1467 near Moscow.[147]

19. Vladimir and Theodosius, Sons of Dionysius of Moscow (1530-1540)

Vladimir and Theodosius, the two sons of Dionysius, painted with their father as members of his cooperative. We know that Theodosius continued to paint after the death of his father; he decorated the Annunciation Cathedral in Moscow in 1508.[148]

20. Andrei Lavrentiev, Ivan Dermayartzev, Ananias and Evstafi Stefanov (1550-1600)

Besides the growing importance of the Moscow school, these painters became known for their works in Novgorod.[149]

21. Procopi Chirin, the Tsar's Iconographer; Istoma and Nicephorus Savin; Nazary Istomin (1580-1600)

The icons painted in what is called the Stroganov style, that is, rather small and delicate miniatures, were very popular at the turn of the 16th century. They are associated with the court of Boris Godunov. The above-mentioned artists were part of the Stroganov school.[150]

22. Longinus of Pec, Monk (1563-1597)

Longinus was a Serbian poet as well as a very well-educated, talented iconographer. Since he signed his works, we are able to follow his career.[151]

23. The Monk George Mitrofanovich, Kosma, Fr. Strahinja of Budimlye, Basil, Mitrophanes, Andrei Raicevich, and Radul of Serbia (1600-1690)

Mitrofanovich was a Serbian iconographer in the

Athonite monastery of Chilandar. He painted icons and frescoes in Serbia and in his monastery on Mount Athos. The paintings that he signed date from 1616-1620, but he was active until 1622. Kosma imitated Longinus' style. Strahinja, Basil, and Mitrophanes were contemporaries of Mitrofanovich and Kosma, though less gifted. Raicevich and Radul painted at the end of the classical period of Serbian icons. After 1690, when the great migration toward Austria took place, the authenticity of the tradition was lost when artists imitated Western European art. The above-mentioned artists, on the other hand, refused all influence from the West and concentrated on the perpetuation of traditional Serbian iconography.[152]

24. Semion Spiridonov, Guiri Nikitin, Sila Savin, and Theodore Zubov (1658)

After the 1658 fire that ravaged the city of Yaroslav, these four artists helped paint the new stone churches.[153]

25. Sister Jeanne Reitlinger (1897-1987)

Sister Jeanne was a teacher and iconographer during the Russian emigration. She taught iconography to George Kroug when the two of them were in Paris around 1933. After 1955, she worked in Tashkent, the Soviet Union.[154]

26. Sister Juliana Sokolova (20th century)

Maria Sokolova gave herself to iconography when she was a young girl and worked all her life to spread the knowledge of canonical iconography. After 1957, she taught in the Moscow Ecclesiastical Academy and the Moscow Seminary. In her works, she made visible what she taught.[155]

27. Archbishop Sergius Goblutzov (beginning of the 20th century)

Archbishop Sergius was one of the founders of the

renewal of canonical iconography, reminding everyone that St. Andrei Rublev and his spirituality are the models to imitate. His work, *The Theological Ideas in the Work of Andrei Rublev*, expresses his conception of the art of the icon.[156]

NOTES

1. S. Bigham, "Les traditions non néotestamentaires", *Les chrétiens et les images*, Montréal, Québec, Editions Paulines, 1992, p. 66.

2. *Le Synaxaire: Vies des saints de l'Eglise orthodoxe*, tome 4, Thessalonica, Editions To Perivoli tis Panagias, 1987, p. 578. As of the date of publication, four volumes, September-June, have been published, henceforth *Synaxaire* 1, 2, 3 or 4.

3. *Synaxaire* 1, pp. 533-534; also see the Annex, *The Synaxarion of Saint Nicodemus the Hagiorite* vol. 2, Athens, 1868, pp. 125-126; translation by Fr. Antony Athanassiadis.

4. For St. Alipy, see *Kievo-Pecherskii paterik, ili skazaniia o zhitii i podvigakh sviatykh ugodnikov Kievo-Pecherskoi Lavry*, Jordanville, N. Y., Holy Trinity Monastery, 1967, pp. 98-104; English translation in Annex "The Life of Our Venerable Father Alypii the Icon Painter," *The Sacred Art Journal*, 10/1, Thomas Drain, tr., March 1989, pp. 12-18; *Medieval Russia's Epics, Chronicles, and Tales*, Serge A. Zenkovsky, tr. from Russian, New York, E. P. Dutton, 1974, pp. 138-140. See also A. Pochtovy, "St. Alipy—the First Russian Icon-Painter, *The Journal of the Moscow Patriarchate* 1989/7, pp. 17-18; Elisabeth Behr-Sigel, "Etudes d'Hagiographie russe", *Irénikon* XII/1935, pp. 241-254.

5. Vladimir Ivanov, *Le grand livre des icônes russes*, Paris, Desclée-Patriarcat de Moscou, 1987, p. 21, henceforth Ivanov.

6. Leonid Ouspensky, *Theology of the Icon*, vol. II, Anthony Gythiel, tr., Crestwood, NY, St. Vladimir's Seminary Press, 1992, p. 254, henceforth Ouspensky.

7. *Zhitiia russkykh sviatykh* II, Jordanville, New York, Holy Trinity Russian Orthodox Monastery, 1984, p. 91, henceforth *Zhitiia*.

8. *Zhitiia* II, pp. 348-352.

9. *The Chronicle of Novgorod: 1016-1471*, R. Michell and N. Forbes, trs., New York, AMS Press, 1970, p. 116, henceforth *Chronicle*.

10. *Ibid.*, p. 124.

11. Engelina Smirnova, *Icônes de l'école de Moscou: XIVe-XVII siècles,* Leningrad, Editions d'art Aurora, 1989, pp. 2 and 151, henceforth Smirnova; Ivanov, pp. 34-35; *Synaxaire* 2, pp. 195-196.

12. *Chronicle,* pp. 126-145.

13. Ivanov, p. 36.

14. *Zhitiia* I, p. 109; *Synaxaire* 3, p. 98.

15. *Calendrier liturgique orthodoxe,* Paris, Fraternité orthodoxe en Europe occidentale, 1994, p. 64. Another liturgical calendar of the Russian tradition, that of the Orthodox Church in America, does not call him iconographer; see *Liturgical Calendar and Rubrics for the Year 1990,* South Canaan, PA., St. Tikhon's Seminary Press, 1990, p. 105.

16. *Synaxaire* 1, pp. 617-618.

17. *Zhitiia* II, pp. 299-301.

18. "The Life and Works of the Venerable Andrei Rublov", *The Canonization of Saints,* Moscow, Publications of the Moscow Patriarchate, 1988, pp. 51-59.

19. Bishop Nathanael, "St. Andrei Roublev", *Orthodox Life,* vol. 28, 1978/5, pp. 1-5.

20. *Troïtskaïa Letopis'* [*The Troitskaya Chronicle*], M. D. Priselkov, ed., Moscow-Leningrad, 1950, p. 459, in Mango, *The Art of the Byzantine Empire: 312-1453,* Toronto, Ont., Medieval Academy of America, 1986, p. 256, henceforth *The Troitskaya Chronicle.*

21. Boris Brodsky, "Le Musée d'art russe ancien Andreï Roublev", *Les trésors artistiques de Moscou,* Moscow, Editions Izobrazitelnoïé Iskousstvo, 1991, pp. 72-89.

22. *La vie de saint Serge,* "Saint André Roublev et Daniel le Noir au monastère Andronikov", *Le Messager orthodoxe,* 1983/ I, #92, p. 97.

23. S. Ostrogorsky, "Les décisions du 'Stoglav' concernant la peinture d'images et les principes de l'iconographie byzantine", *Byzanz und die Welt der Slawen,* Darmstadt, Wissenschaftliche Buchgesellschaft, 1974, p. 130, quoted in E. Duchesne, *Le Stoglav or les Cent chapitres, recueil des décisions de l'assemblée ecclésiastique de Moscou 1551,* Paris, Bibliothèque de l'Institut français de Pétrograd, 1920.

24. V. Lebedev, "St. Andrei Roublev", *The Journal of the Moscow Patriarchate*, 1989/7, pp. 43-44; Ivanov, pp. 60-69; Smirnova, pp. 13-33. We have not been able to find a reference to Andrei Rublev in Dionysius of Fourna, *The Painter's Manual of Dionysius of Fourna*, Paul Hetherington, tr., London, The Sagittarius Press, 1981, henceforth *The Painter's Manual;* or in *An Iconographer's Patternbook: The Stroganov Tradition*, Christopher Kelly, tr., Torrance, CA, Oakwood Publications, 1992.

25. Alvida Mirzoyan, *Grigor Tatevatsi and an Anonymous Painter of Syuniq*, Yerevan, Sovetakan Grogh Publishing House, 1987, pp. 30-32; thanks to Arminé Keuchgerian for her help.

26. *Zhitiia* I, pp. 255-258.

27. *Synaxaire* 4, pp. 416-417.

28. N. Kalogeropoulos, *Metabyzantine kai veoellenike texne*, in Greek, Athens, 1926, Photios Kontoglou, *Explanation of Orthodox Iconography* I [in Greek], Athens 1992, p. 41; Phoibos Piombinos, *Hellenes Agiographoi Mexri to 1821* [Greek Iconographers up to 1821], Society of Greek Literature and Historical Archives, Athens, 1979, p. 72; see *Synaxaire* 2, pp. 493-496.

29. *The Collection of Russian Chronicles*, vol. 4/sect. 1, Leningrad, 1929, p. 544 in Archm. Makary, "The Life of St. Makary, Metropolitan of Moscow and All Russia", *The Journal of the Moscow Patriarchate* 6/1989, p. 55.

30. *Ibid.* vol. 13/ sect. 1, p. 254 in "The Life ... ", p. 59.

31. Bishop Dimitri Sambikin, *Mesyatseslov svyatykh, vseyu Russkoyu Tserkoviyu ili mestno chtimyky* [Menologion of Saints Venerated by the Whole Russian Church or Only Locally], Kamenets-Podolsk, 1895, p. 216 in "The Life ... ", p. 60.

32. "The Story of the Life of St. Makary, Metropolitan of Moscow", *The Journal of the Moscow Patriarchate* 6/1989, pp. 54-65.

33. For the role of the Metropolitan in the controversy over the image of God the Father, see S. Bigham, "Three Russian Councils", *The Image of God the Father*, Torrance, Calif., Oakwood Publications, pp. 51-60; Ouspensky, pp. 303-323; and Ivanov, pp. 77-97. The point of view expressed by the Metropolitan in his justification of the image of God the Father continues to create controversy.

While we do not share the opinion of the metropolitan, but rather that expressed by Viskovaty, we simply note that a person's holiness is no guarantee against questionable opinions. Even though we must respect everyone's opinions, we are not obliged to accept them, even when a holy metropolitan expresses them. As St. Photius the Great said about St. Augustine: "Even though we know that certain of our fathers and doctors have deviated from the faith on certain dogmas, we do not receive as doctrine those points in which they deviated. We nonetheless continue to embrace them as men.". (*Ep.* 24, 20, PG 102, 813) *Synaxaire* 4, note 18, p. 559.

34. *Synaxaire* 3, pp. 304-305. See *Zhitiia* I, pp. 148-150 which gives March 4 as the date of his feast but mentions nothing of his iconographic activity.

35. *Zhitiia* I, pp. 133-134.

36. *Synaxaire* 3, pp. 188-189.

37. *Synaxaire* 4, p. 578.

38. *Zhitiia* I, p. 281.

39. Ivan Bogdanov, *Bezemertni slova* [Eternal Words], Sophia, 1980, pp. 226-230.

40. Atanas Bozhkov, *Bulgarian Icons*, Sofia, Bulgarski Houdoazhnik Publishers, 1987, pp. 122-123.

41. *Synaxaire* 3, p. 17. The notice for Sts. Anastasius in Saints Macarios of Corinth and Nicodemus the Hagiorite, *The Synaxarion of New Martyrs*, Thessalonica, Editions Orthodoxas Kipsela, 1984, pp. 269-270, translation by Fr. Antony Athanassiadis.

42. *Synaxaire* 4, p. 77. See the *Life of St. Iorest* in the Annex: Hieromonk Ioanichie Balan, *Pateric Românesc*, Bucharest, Editura Institutului Biblic si de Misiune al Bisericii Ortodoxe Române, 1980, pp. 137-138, translated from Romanian by Horia Roscanu.

43. The notice of St. Joseph in *The Synaxarion of New Martyrs*, p. 753, translation by Fr. Antony Athanassiadis.

44. *Synaxaire* 3, pp. 566-569; C. Cavarnos, *St. Savvas the New*, Belmont, Mass., Institute for Byzantine and Modern Greek Studies, 1985.

45. "Saint Theodosia, Virgin Martyr," *Orthodox Life*, 1984/3, pp. 29-30; *Synaxaire* 4, p. 393.

46. *Synaxaire métrique et tables du ménée*, Denis Guillaume, tr., Rome, Diaconie apostolique, 1991, p. 199.

47. *Synaxaire métrique*, p. 64.

48. A. Labate, "Germain de Constantinople," *Dictionnaire encyclopédique du christianisme ancien*, t. 1, pp. 1041-1043; *Synaxaire* 4, pp. 246-249.

49. *Synaxaire* 3, p. 236.

50. *Ibid.*, p. 242.

51. *Ibid.*, p. 413.

52. *Ibid.*, p. 467.

53. *Synaxaire* 1, pp. 612-615. According to the information given by Sp. Lamprou II ("Greek Iconographers Before the Fall of Constantinople," in Greek, *Neos Ellenomnémon* V, 1908, pp. 270-289), Piombinos, p. 239, calls St. Stephen the Younger *iconographer*. We have not been able to confirm this in any other source, including two Greek synaxaria.

54. *Ibid.*, pp. 615-616.

55. *Menée de novembre*, "Canon pour saint Etienne le jeune," Denis Guillaume, tr., Rome Diaconie apostolique, 1983, p. 325.

56. *Ibid.*; *Synaxaire* 3, p. 394.

57. *Synaxaire* 1, p. 306.

58. *Synaxaire* 2, p. 130.

59. *Synaxaire* 1, pp. 264-265.

60. See *The Synaxarion of St. Nicodemus the Hagiorite*, Athens, 1868, for the date indicated.

61. *Synaxaire* 3, pp. 393-394.

62. *Synaxaire* 3, pp. 536-540.

63. *Synaxaire* 2, p. 265.

64. *Synaxaire* 3, pp. 348-350.

65. See *The Synaxarion of St. Nicodemus the Hagiorite*, Athens, 1868, for the date indicated.

66. *Synaxaire* 4, p. 27.

67. *Synaxaire* 3, pp. 565-566.

68. *Synaxaire* 1, p. 93.

69. *Synaxaire* 3, p. 525.

70. *Synaxaire* 4, p. 196.

71. *Synaxaire* 3, pp. 196-197.

72. *Synaxaire* 4, pp. 347-350.

73. *Synaxaire* 3, p. 321.

74. *Synaxaire* 1, pp. 286-287.

75. *Synaxaire* 3, pp. 319-321.

76. *Synaxaire* 2, pp. 249-250.

77. *Synaxaire* 3, pp. 510-512.

78. *Synaxaire* 4, p. 31.

79. *Synaxaire* 1, pp. 268-270.

80. *Synaxaire* 2, pp. 155-157.

81. *Synaxaire* 4, pp. 537-541.

82. *Synaxaire* 4, p. 121.

83. *Synaxaire* 3, pp. 374-375.

84. *Synaxaire* 3, p. 420.

85. *Synaxaire* 3, pp. 478-479.

86. *Synaxaire* 3, p. 598.

87. *Synaxaire* 3, p. 458.

88. *Synaxaire* 4, p. 30.

89. *Synaxaire* 4, p. 37.

90. *Synaxaire* 4, p. 255.

91. *Synaxaire* 4, p. 380.

92. *Synaxaire* 3, pp. 34-37.

93. J. Gouillard, "Grégoire II et l'iconoclasme," *Travaux et Mémoires* 3, Paris, Editions E. De Boccard, 1968, pp. 276-305.

94. John of Damascus, *On the Divine Images*, Crestwood, New York, St. Vladimir's Seminary Press, 1980.

95. *Synaxaire* 2, pp. 40-43.

96. *Synaxaire* 3, pp. 223-226.

97. *Synaxaire* 1, pp. 274-277.

98. *Discours contre les iconoclastes*, Marie-José Mondzain-Baudinet, tr., Paris, Editions Klincksieck, 1989; *Synaxaire* 4, pp. 418-423.

99. *Synaxaire* 1, pp. 481-486.

100. *Synaxaire* 3, pp. 103-105.

101. The word *master* supposes a value judgment, an appreciation of the high artistic quality of a work. In the case of certain artists discussed below, the definitive evaluation of their works as icons has yet to be made.

102. V. N. Lazarev, *Theophanes the Greek and His School,* [in Russian], Moscow, 1961, pp. 113 ff.; see Mango, pp. 256-258.

103. *Ibid.,* p. 113, quoted in Ouspensky II, p. 261.

104. *The Third Novgorod Chronicle,* A. F. Byckov, ed., Saint-Petersburg, 1897, p. 243 in Mango, p. 256.

105. *The Troitskaya Chronicle,* p. 445, in Mango, p. 256.

106. *Ibid.,* p. 450, in Mango, p. 256.

107. *Ibid.,* p. 459, in Mango, p. 256; also see Ouspensky II, note 48, pp. 273-274; Smirnova, pp. 10-13; Ivanov, pp. 58-60.

108. *The Painter's Manual,* p. 2.

109. Weitzmann et al, *The Icon,* New York, Alfred A. Knopf 1982, pp. 134-135, 137, 140-141; C. Cavarnos, *Byzantine Thought and Art,* Belmont, Mass., Institute for Byzantine and Modern Greek Studies,1968, pp. 79-84; Cavarnos, *Anchored in God,* Belmont, Mass., Institute for Byzantine and Modern Greek Studies,1968, pp. 33-42; Ouspensky II, note 31, pp. 231-251.

110. "Saint André Roublev et Daniel le Noir au monastère Andronikov", *Le Messager orthodoxe,* 1983/ I, #92, p. 97.

111. *Synaxaire* 1, p. 536.

112. Leonid Ouspensky and Vladimir Lossky,*The Meaning of Icons,* Crestwood, NY, St. Vladimir's Seminary Press, 1982, pp. 46-47.

113. V. Lebedev, "St. Andrei Rublev", *The Journal of the Moscow Patriarchate,* 1989/7, pp. 43-44; Bishop Nathanael, "St. Andrei Rublev", *Orthodox Life,* 1978/#5, vol. 28, pp. 1-5.

114. *The Chronicle of Moscow* quoted in Valentin Bulkin, *Dionysius,* Leningrad, Aurora Art Publishers, 1982, p. 4, henceforth *Dionysius.*

115. *Ibid.*

116. Ouspensky II, p. 273.

117. Ivanov, pp. 69-74; Ouspensky II, pp. 263-275; Irina Kyzlassova, *L'icône russe XIVe-XVIe siècles,* Leningrad, Editions d'art Aurora, 1988, pp. 16-19; Engelina Smirnova, *Icônes de l'école de Moscou: XIVe-XVIIe siècles,* Leningrad, Editions d'art Aurora, 1989, pp. 33-38.

118. Weitzmann, pp. 312-313; Kalokyris, pp. 175-178.

119. *The Painter's Manual;* C. Cavarnos, *The Holy Mountain,* Belmont, Mass., Institute for Byzantine and Modern Greek Studies, 1973, pp. 27-28.

120. Ouspensky II, pp. 329-349; Mikhail Syrchin, "The Icon-Painter Simon Ushakov and the Russian Art of the 17th Century" 1 &2, *The Journal of the Moscow Patriarchate,* 12/1986 pp. 63-66 and 1/1987 pp. 69-72; Ivanov, pp. 110-150.

121. Ivanov, pp. 110-111; Ouspensky II, pp. 329-349.

122. "Avant-Propos", *Le Messager orthodoxe* 112, 1989/III, pp. 1-8; *The Journal of the Moscow Patriarchate,* 1988/II, pp. 23-24; J.-R. Bouchet, F.-D. Boespflug,"Léonide Ouspensky, iconographe, théologien: notre ami", *Messager de l'exarchat du Patriarche russe en Europe occidentale,* 1985/#114, pp. 11-14.

123. N. Ozzoline, "In memoriam Léonide Ouspensky", *Le Messager orthodoxe,* #112, 1989/111, p. 7; see also *Byzantine Thought and Art,* pp. 73-78; C. Cavarnos, *Orthodox Iconography,* Belmont, Mass., Institute for Byzantine and Modern Greek Studies, 1980, pp. 55-59, *Byzantine Sacred Art,* 1983 and *Meetings with Kontoglou,* 1992.

124. Ivanov, p. 200; *The Journal of the Moscow Patriarchate,* 1970/3; G. I. Krug, *Carnets d'un peintre d'icônes,* Lausanne, L'Age d'Homme, 1983, pp. 7-30; A. Tregubov, *The Light of Christ: Iconography of Gregory Kroug,* Crestwood, N. Y., Saint Vladimir's Seminary Press, 1990.

125. *Bulgarian Icons,* pp. 70-71.

126. According to information given by Kontoglou, p. 417, Piombinos, p. 161, calls Methodius *saint.* The Bulgarian Church does not include Methodius among its saints, and we have not been able to confirm this designation elsewhere.

127. Weitzmann, p. 135.

128. *Ibid.,* pp. 137-138.

129. Vera Laourina, Vassili Pouchkariov, *Les icônes russes: école*

de Novgorod XIIe-XVIIe siècles, Leningrad, Editions d'art Aurora, 1983, pp. 23-24.

130. L. M. Yevseyeva, I. A. Kochetkov, V. N. Sergeyev, *Early Tver Painting,* Moscow, Iskusstvo Publications, 1974, pp. 12-13; Olga Popova, *Russian Illuminated Manuscripts,* London, Thames and Hudson, 1984, #17.

131. *Chronicle,* pp. 131 and 133.

132. *The Troitskaya Chronicle,* p. 366, in Mango, p. 256.

133. Ivanov, p. 55.

134. Weitzmann, p. 142.

135. *The Troitskaya Chronicle,* p. 445, in Mango, p. 256.

136. Weitzmann, p. 143.

137. M. Alpatov et I. Rodnikova, *Icônes-Pskov XIIe-XVIe Siècles,* Leningrad, Aurore Editions d'Art, 1991, p. 24, quoted in a book by Gorski, 1859, pp. 191-192, see the bibliography p. 320. See Ouspensky II, p. 318 and Ivanov, pp. 40-42.

138. *The Troitskaya Chronicle,* p. 459, in Mango, p. 256.

139. Alpatov, pp. 42-44; Ivanov, p. 78; Ouspensky II, pp. 303-323.

140. Alpatov, p. 26.

141. See S. Bigham, *The Image of God the Father,* "The Three Russian Councils", Torrance, CA, Oakwood Publications, 1995, pp. 51-60.

142. Gregory Kroug, *Carnets d'un peintre d'icônes,* Lausanne, Editions l'Age d'Homme, 1983, pp. 51-85.

143. *Ibid.,* p. 85.

144. Konstantin Kalokyris, *The Byzantine Wall Paintings of Crete,* New York, Red Dust, 1973, pp. 31-33.

145. Weitzmann, pp. 310-315.

146. *Dionysius,* p. 4.

147. *Ibid.*

148. *Ibid.*

149. Ivanov, p. 96.

150. *Ibid.,* pp. 96-101; Smirnova, pp. 42-45; Anna Vicini et al, *Symbols of Glory: The Stroganov Icons,* Middle Green, UK, St. Paul MultiMedia Productions UK, 1992.

151. Weitzmann, pp. 306-308.

152. *Ibid.*, pp. 308-309.

153. S. I. Maslenitsyn,*Yaroslavian Icon-Painting* Moscow, Iskusstvo Publishers, 1973, pp. 35 ff.; Ivanov, pp. 121-125.

154. A. Vedernikov, *The Journal of the Moscow Patriarchate,* 1989/5, p. 17.

155. Ivanov, pp. 200-202.

156. *Ibid.*, pp. 199-200.

The Annex: The Lives of the Saints in Translation

1. Saint Lazarus the Iconographer

St. Lazarus became a monk and learned iconography when he was still very young. He gave himself to ascetical exercises and to continence, especially to alms-giving for which he was judged worthy to be made a priest. From then on, he fought all kinds of heresies. As a result, he underwent much hardship and unimaginable sufferings at the hands of the Nestorians and the disciples of Eutyches and Dioscorus, but mainly the iconoclasts. He was sent on a mission to Old Rome in order to help defend the dogmas of the fathers and the apostles, which were being attacked by those who denigrated the holy icons. Upon returning to Constantinople with great honor, he was again sent to Rome for another mission. En route, the weather changes made him sick. He gave up his soul to God, and some time later, his holy body was transferred to the monastery named after St. Evandria.

2. The Life of Our Venerable Father Alipy the Icon Painter

Our venerable Father Alipy of the Caves Monastery [in Kiev] was an imitator of the holy Evangelist, St. Luke. This holy man, who so marvelously depicted the likenesses of the saints in icons, was himself a great doer of good works and at the same time a wondrous healer.

In the days of the pious prince of Kiev, Vsevolod Yaroslavich, when St. Nikon was abbot, by the providence of God and at the invitation of SS. Anthony and Theodosius, Greek Iconographers came to the Monastery of the Caves from the city of Constantinople. St. Alipy was sent by his parents to these artists to learn the art of painting icons. While working with them, he was an eye-witness of that most wonderful miracle which is narrated in our account of the monastery church when, during the painting of the sanctuary, the icon of the most holy Mother of God appeared of itself, shining like the sun; and a dove, flying out of her mouth, after flying about for a long time, flew into the mouth of the image of the Savior. From this time on, St. Alipy was assured that the Holy Spirit would abide in the Church of the Caves Monastery. After the work of adorning the monastery church with icons was completed, St. Alipy took the monastic habit from the Venerable St. Nikon the Abbot, and continued more and more to perfect his art. By painting the likenesses of these holy persons, he, by the grace of God, was able to show in material images the beneficent countenances of the saints. For he had taken up the art of icon painting not for the sake of amassing riches, but for the sake of virtue. He painted icons free of charge for everyone, both the abbot and the brethren. The holy monk spent special efforts on the restoration of damaged icons of the monastery church. If it happened that he was unable to fulfill any commission, he returned the gold and silver which had been prepared for the work, sometimes paying with icons those to whom such repayment was due. He was never idle, and in this he imitated the holy monks of antiquity, who worked with their hands, and the greatest apostle, Paul himself, who said, "You all know that these hands of mine earned enough for the needs of myself and my companions" (Acts 20:34).

Whenever Alipy earned anything by his work, he divided the money into three portions. The first he put aside to purchase necessary materials for icons; the second, to be distributed to the poor; and the third, for the needs of the monastery. This was his way of life, never giving himself repose, day or night, praying and making prostrations. When day broke, then in all humility, purity of heart, patience, fasting, love, and constant remembrance of God, he took up his work once more. No one ever saw him idle, and he never failed to attend the church offices with full attention. The abbot of the monastery noticed what virtuous art there was with this venerable icon-painter who, being in the monastic-angelic state, was worthy to exhibit in himself the action of the consubstantial image of the Son—Jesus Christ, a priest according to the order of Melchizedek. Seeing all of this, the abbot decided to advance him to the rank of the priesthood. Then the venerable monk, like a lamp set upon a lamp stand—or I will go further and say, like an image hung on high—shone with the double glory of monastic virtue and priestly beauty. He was no common example of this state, but was truly a wonder-worker.

We cannot omit to tell here of a few examples of his wonder-working. There was a certain rich man of Kiev who was stricken with leprosy. He desperately sought help from both doctors and magical healers and frequently went to see them all. He even consulted healers who were of other religious faiths, but he received no help from them, and his illness worsened. Then, one of his friends suggested he go to the Monastery of the Caves and ask help of the fathers there. He had very little confidence in such advice and set out for the monastery almost against his will. When he had been led there, the abbot told him to drink some water from the well of St. Theodosius and to wash his head and face with it. When he followed these instructions, every ulcer produced a frightful inflammation in the body of the leper, and an unbearable stench repulsed everyone around him. All this took place as the result of his lack of faith. Returning in such condition to his home, the leper began to weep and lament. For many days, he would not appear in public because he was ashamed of the stench, and he said to his friends, "Shame hath covered my face. I am become a stranger to my brethren, and an alien to the sons of my mother (Ps. 68: 8-9), since I went without faith to the

Venerable Fathers Anthony and Theodosius."

In such distress and bitterness, he daily awaited his death. Then, all of a sudden, he came to his senses and decided to confess all his sins. So, for this reason, he went to the Venerable Fr. Alipy at the Monastery of the Caves and made his confession to him. The saint said to him, "You have done well, my son, to confess your sins to God in my unworthy presence, for thus does the prophet testify of himself, calling out to the Lord, 'I said, I will confess against myself mine iniquity unto the Lord, and thou hast forgiven the wickedness of my sin' (Ps. 31:9)." Then he gave him much instruction about the salvation of his soul and, taking some color that he used for the icons, he painted his face with it, anointing his festering sores. Then he led him into the church, gave him Holy Communion, and instructed him to wash with the water with which the priests were accustomed to purify themselves after receiving the Holy Eucharist. In working this miracle, our Venerable Fr. Alipy showed himself to be most Christ-like. For just as Christ, when he healed the leper, ordered him to show himself to the priests and to offer a gift for his cleansing, so this saint ordered his leper to show himself to persons of priestly rank and to offer a gift, concerning which the prophet says, "What shall I offer to the Lord for all he hath given me? I will take the cup of salvation" (Ps. 115: 3-4). Regarding the gift, let us record here that the great-grandson of the leper vowed a golden canopy over the altar in the Caves Monastery church.

Moreover, the saint showed himself an imitator of Christ, who healed the man born blind. For, just as Christ, in healing him, first anointed his eyes with spittle and then ordered him to wash in the Pool of Siloam (John. 9:7 ff), so the saint first anointed the leper's sores with the paints he used for icons, and then ordered him to wash with the water which had been used by the priests to wash after Communion. And thus he healed the man from his illness and at the same time from spiritual blindness.

This instant healing completely amazed those who had come from the city together with the leper. But St. Alipy said to them, "Brethren, heed what is said: 'No man can serve two masters' (Matt. 6:24). Now this man had formerly given himself over by sin to the Deceiver and afterwards came here ill-advised, despairing of his salvation, and not believing in the Lord, the only Savior. For this reason, his illness worsened and came upon him with still greater force, because of his disbelief. When the Lord said 'Ask, and it shall be given to you' (Matt. 7:7), he meant not an ordinary asking, but a request made with faith. And now you see that when this leper turned in repentance to God for his sin of disbelief, and did what I ordered, God, rich in his mercy, has healed him."

When they had heard this, the people prostrated themselves on the ground and departed with the leper, praising God and his Mother, together with our Venerable Fathers Anthony and Theodosius, and their venerable disciple, our Fr. Alipy, about whom they said, "Truly he is a new Elisha who cured this man of leprosy, as Elisha cured Naaman the Syrian" (2 Kings 5: 1-14).

In that same city of Kiev, there was another Christ-loving man who had built a church and wished to adorn it with seven large icons. He gave some money for this purpose to two monks of the Monastery of the Caves with whom he was acquainted. He also gave them panels of wood for the icons, asking them to confer about painting such icons with the monk Alipy. These two monks said nothing of this to Alipy, but kept the money for themselves.

A certain amount of time passed, and the client sent to the monks to inquire whether the icons had been painted. They replied that Alipy wanted more money. The client sent more money, and the monks kept this sum, as well. Then these shameless monks, casting further lies on the saint, sent to the client saying that Alipy demanded as much money again as he had already receive. The Christ-loving man gave them money a third time, saying "My desire is to have the prayers and blessings that come from the work of his hands." (Now Alipy was still completely ignorant of the actions of these two monks.) Following this, the man sent to inquire whether the icons were finished. The monks, not knowing what to answer, informed him that although Alipy had taken triple the price of the icons, he absolutely refused to paint them. At this point that Christ-loving man came to the Caves Monastery with a large retinue and went to the Venerable Abbot Nikon and informed him of the fraudulent action of Alipy. The abbot, summoning the saint, said, "What is the purpose, brother, of such injustice to our son? Numerous times he has requested you to paint the icons, and gave you all the money you asked. What then, brother, is the meaning of this? For you are the one who sometimes paints icons for free!"

Alipy answered him, "Honorable Father, your Holiness knows that I have never been lazy about my work, but now, I don't know what you are talking about."

The abbot told him the whole story of how he had taken triple the price for the seven icons and as yet he had not painted them. Then, to convict the saint, the abbot immediately ordered the panels for those icons to be brought forward. The day before, these panels had been seen in one of the monastery storerooms, completely unpainted. The abbot also ordered that the monks through whose hands the money was given to the saint should be made to appear. The monks were summoned as witnesses against Alipy. Those who had been sent to fetch the panels went into the storeroom and found instead of the empty panels, finished icons, painted with great taste.

They brought them to the abbot and the assembled people. Everyone was stricken with awe and fell down trembling, with their faces to the floor, in veneration of these icons not painted by human hands: the images of the Lord, his Most Pure Mother, and his saints. After this, the two monks who had slandered Alipy came in and, unaware of the miracle that had taken place, they began to contend with the saint, saying that he had taken three times the price and still had not painted the icons. When they had heard this attack, everyone present showed the icons to those monks and said, "You see, these icons have now been painted by God himself as a testimony of Alipy's innocence." When they realized what a miracle had occurred, they were terrified.

Immediately after this, the abbot defrocked those monks and expelled them from the monastery for their wicked thievery and for their lies. But even this did not stop their evil deeds, for they began to spread their slander against Alipy, saying throughout the whole city that they had painted those icons themselves. Their story was that they had worked for Alipy and that he did not want to pay them. Instead, they said, he had taken their money and concocted a lie about the icons, giving it out that the icons had been painted by God himself, as if to vindicate Alipy. And in this way, the monks attempted to turn the people against those icons. The people actually believed the monks who slandered St. Alipy. But God glorifies his saints, as he says himself in the Gospels: "A City seated on a mount cannot be hid. Neither do men light a candle and put in under a bushel, but on a candlestick that it may shine to all that are in the house." (Matt. 5: 14) So the Lord did not conceal the virtuous efforts of this righteous man; and the miracle of those icons, performed for the sake of the saint, came to the attention of Prince Vladimir Monomakh, and was confirmed by the following occurrence.

It happened that, in the providence of God, there was a fire in Kiev, and the entire district of Podol' burned, including the church in which those icons were kept. After the fire, however, the icons were discovered to be intact and undamaged. When the prince learned of this, he came himself to behold such a miracle. And when he saw the intact icons and heard how they had been painted in one night by the hand of God himself, the Defender of St. Alipy, then Vladimir Monomakh glorified God who had worked such a wonder for the sake of St. Alipy. The prince took one of the icons—the image of the most holy Mother of God—and sent it to the city of Rostov, to be placed in a stone church which he himself had built. As it happened, however, that church building collapsed, but the icon survived undamaged. Then it was moved to a wooden church, but that church soon burned. Once again, the icon survived untouched without showing even the least sign of having been in a fire. All of this testifies to the virtuous life of St. Alipy, for whose sake these icons not made by human hands had been created.

Let us go now to the miracle which preceded the death of the saint, as this man, a wonder-working painter of images, made in the image of God, moved from temporal life to the eternal.

A certain pious man gave a commission to Alipy to paint an icon of the Dormition of the Most Holy Mother of God for a church by that name, and requested that the icon be completed for the Feast of the Dormition. A few days later, St. Alipy fell ill and, approaching his own mortal dormition, was unable to fulfill the commission, so the icon remained unpainted. The client was disappointed and became indignant with the saint, but Alipy said to him, "My child, don't bring your sorrow to me, but cast your sorrow on the Lord, and he will do as he sees fit. The icon will stand in its place for the feast." The man believed the words of the saint and returned rejoicing to his home. When he came back to see Alipy, it was already the Vigil of the Feast of the Most Holy Mother of God, and seeing the icon unfinished and St. Alipy even more seriously ill, he began to berate him saying, "Why didn't you tell me that you were too weak to finish the work so that I could have had another icon-painter make the image, and the feast would be celebrated properly and respectfully? But now you are disgracing me." The saint answered him briefly, "My son, do you think I am acting out of laziness? Keep in mind that God is able to paint the icons of his Mother by his word alone. As for me, I am departing this world, as God has revealed to me, but I will not leave you sorrowing." The man left in deepest sorrow. But after he left, a certain radiant youth came to St. Alipy and began to paint the icon. Alipy, thinking that in his anger the client had sent another painter, marveled at his ability to paint icons. But the speed and beauty of the work showed that it was an angel painting, since the artist produced a wonderful icon in three hours, including gilding, grinding the various colors on the stone, and painting. Then he said to the saint, "Father, what remains to be done here, and where have I made any mistakes?"

"You have done well," Alipy answered, "God has helped you paint so beautifully. In fact, he has painted it himself."

When evening came, the painter and the icon disappeared. The man who had ordered the icon spent the entire night in sorrow that the icon would not be ready for the feast. When morning came, he arose and went to the church to weep there for his sin, as a consequence of which the church would be without an icon for the feast of the Dormition. But when he opened the doors, he saw the icon standing in its place, radiant with light. Then he fell down out of fear thinking he was having some kind of vision. But when he raised himself up a little and looked closely, he saw that it was a real icon. Then with fear and trembling, he remembered the words of St. Alipy, who said that the icon would be ready for the feast. With great joy, he returned home and informed his household. They joyfully hurried to the church with candles and censers, and seeing the icon shining like the sun, they fell with their foreheads to the ground in prostrations, and kissed the icon with rejoicing. Afterwards, that pious man went to the abbot to tell him of the miracle with the icon. Then everyone went to see St. Alipy, but the saint was already departing this world. The abbot asked him, "Father, when and by whom was the icon painted for this man?" Alipy related all that he had seen, saying that an angel had painted it, "and even now he is standing before me, preparing to take me with him." Having said this, the saint gave up his soul into the hands of the Lord on the seventeenth day of the month of August (1114 A. D.). The brethren washed his body and carried it into the church, and when they had sung the customary service over him, they buried him in the caves of St. Anthony. And so this holy and wonder-working icon-painter adorned both heaven and earth—the heavens by his virtuous soul, and the earth with his pure body.

This account was written in honor of iconographers, to the glory of God the Father and First Principle, who said, "Let us make man in our image and likeness," and also in the image of God the Son, who took on the form of a man, together with the Holy Spirit, who descended in the forms of a dove and of tongues of fire — the Trinity, one in substance, whom together with the Venerable Fr. Alipy, we are made worthy to praise for endless ages of ages. Amen.

English translation by Thomas Drain.

3. The Arrival of Greek Iconographers in Kiev

Ten years after the time when by the will and power of the most pure Mother of God the builders of the Pechersk church were sent from Constantinople, icon painters, again from Constantinople, came to Nikon, the abbot of Pechersk and addressed him with these remarkable words: "Show us those men who made the agreement with us regarding the decoration of the church with icons. We want to come to some reckoning with them since during our negotiations they showed us a small church to be decorated with icons, whereas this church is very large. Or take back the gold given us during the negotiations and we will return to Constantinople." The abbot understood nothing of what he had heard from the icon painters and asked, "How did they look, these men who made the agreement with you?" The icon painters described their appearance and their faces, and added that one of those who had made the agreement with them was called Anthony and the other Theodosius. Then the abbot answered them briefly: "O my sons, we cannot show you these men, since it is already more than ten years since they have departed to God and now they ceaselessly pray for us, protecting this church, defending this monastery and caring for those who live the ascetic life in it." The iconographers were struck with wonder at such an answer. They produced many witnesses, in whose presence the agreement had been made, and said to the abbot: "In the presence of these people the monks we named made the agreement with us and in their presence we received gold from the hands of those monks, and you do not want to show them to us. If they are already dead, show us their likenesses so that we and the witnesses can see if it were they." Then the abbot, before all those present, brought out the icon of the venerable Anthony and Theodosius of the Caves. When they saw the image, the iconographers and the witnesses bowed down to the earth and said: "Truly these are the men, and we believe that they are living even after death, and are able to help and protect those who turn to them." Then the witnesses, who were Greek merchants, donated for the work pigments which they had brought to sell. And the iconographers, repenting of their sins, gave the following account of their journey: "When we set out on board ship for the city of Kaneva, then far off on high we beheld a huge church and we asked the people who were there what church it might be. They answered 'It is the church of the Caves Monastery, which you are to decorate. We were very unhappy that the church was so large, and we immediately decided to turn back down the river. That night, a fearful storm came up and our ship sailed back up the river against the current, as if some strange force carried it along, and when morning came we found ourselves at Tripoli. Fear came upon us and for the entire day we wondered what this meant, that in the space of a single night, without rowing, we had covered a distance which ordinarily would take three days. The following night we saw the church again, and in it the patronal icon of the most holy Mother of God, who addressed the following words to us: 'Why, O People, do you vainly oppose the will of my Son and my own? If you do not obey me and sail on downstream, I will take you up and place you in my church, and know that you will not leave, but you will become monks there and end your lives in that monastery, and I will pour out my mercy on your future days at the prayers of the builders, Anthony and Theodosius.' When we arose the next morning we decided to sail downstream nevertheless, but despite our strength, the ship not only did not sail downstream but, on the contrary, sailed upstream against the current, regardless of our efforts to go in the opposite direction. After lengthy and vain attempts we came to our senses and submitted to the will of God, and very soon our ship docked at the monastery walls." When the iconographers had finished their account, all those who had heard it and everyone present there glorified the Lord God and his Most Pure Mother and the venerable Saints Anthony and Theodosius.

The iconographers set themselves to the task of decorating and painting the walls of the church and the Lord himself assisted them with marvelous signs and wonders.

While the iconographers were executing the paintings in the sanctuary of that God-founded church, by miraculous power a wonderful image of the Mother of God appeared in the sanctuary. This miracle took place in the sight of all: the iconographers were all working together inside the sanctuary attending to their tasks. One of the number was a monk of the Monastery of the Caves who was learning the art, the Venerable St. Alypii. Suddenly a miraculous icon of the Mother of God appeared on the wall and when everyone present had turned his wondering gaze on the apparition, the icon suddenly began to shine with an extraordinary light, brighter than the sun, so that it was impossible to gaze upon it and those who beheld this miracle fell to the floor. Afterwards, when they arose, the iconographers began to gaze at the wondrous image once again, when out of the mouth of the Mother of God depicted there, a white dove flew to the icon of the Savior and concealed itself behind the image. Then the dove flew out of the mouth of the Savior and flew about the church, flew up to and alighted on each of the icons of the saints - on the hand of one, on the head of another - and then flew behind the icon of the Mother of God. The iconographers wanted to catch the dove, so they set up a ladder; but when they had mounted the ladder, they found nothing behind the icon and then, searching the entire church, they could not find the dove anywhere. Everyone stood gazing with wonder at the icon which had miraculously appeared in the sanctuary when suddenly the dove flew out of the mouth of the Mother of God once again and flew up to the image of the Savior. The people who were standing below shouted "Catch it!" to the masters who were working above, and they did try to catch it with their outstretched hands, but the dove flew once more into the mouth of the Savior, and the icons began to shine once more with a brilliant light, and the masters who were there once again fell to the floor, bowing before the Savior with heartfelt thanks that they had been granted this vision of the action of the Holy Spirit abiding in the monastery church.

When they had finished the decoration of the church with icons and paintings, the iconographers stayed to live in the Pechersk Lavra, in the practice of prayer, adorning themselves with ascetic exercises and lives of good works. They took the monastic vows themselves and died in that monastery at an advanced age and were buried together with the builders of the monastery in the cave of St. Anthony. Their incorrupt bodies are still venerated as relics here.

And so, the prophecy was fulfilled which these blessed iconographers heard when they desired to turn around and go back to Constantinople and when there appeared to them the church and its most pure icon of the Mother of God, who said to them "Do not leave, but become monks and end your lives there."

English translation by Thomas Drain.

4. Saint Peter the Bishop, Wonderworker of Moscow and All Russia

St. Peter was born about 1260 into a noble family of boyars in Volynia. Before his birth, in a dream, his mother saw herself holding a lamb in her hands, and from between its horns, there grew a tree covered with flowers, fruit, and burning candles. At the age of seven, the boy began to study his letters, without any success until in a dream an unknown man touched his mouth. After this, he began to be a good student.

At the age of twelve, this future bishop entered the monastery. He took as his guide the *Ladder of Perfection* of St. John Climacus, and he was particularly assiduous in humility and obedience. The beginning of his monastic life was especially difficult: he performed very strenuous tasks in the kitchen, worked the land, and washed the hair-shirts of the other monks. During this time, he also studied icon-painting.

After a certain period of experience, his elder gave his blessing for Peter to move to an isolated spot on the banks of the river Rata, where he founded the Monastery of the Transfiguration.

The monastery was visited by Maximus, the metropolitan of All Russia (commemorated on December 6), and Abbot Peter gave him an icon of the Mother of God which he had painted (now called the Petrovskaya icon) and which is preserved even to our own day in the Cathedral of the Dormition in the Moscow Kremlin. A number of other icons he painted have also been preserved.

After the death of Metropolitan Maximus, the question of selecting a new Russian metropolitan arose. Peter had the support of the Prince Yurii Lvovich of Galicia-Volynia, who sent his candidate to Constantinople for appointment. Meanwhile the Grand Duke of Tver and Vladimir proposed his own candidate, Gerontius, abbot of Tver. Abbot Peter arrived in Constantinople first, while Abbot Gerontius was delayed by a storm. During the storm, the Mother of God appeared to Gerontius and told him that Peter should be the metropolitan of Russia. The same message was revealed to Patriarch Athanasius. Metropolitan Peter received the title of Bishop of Kiev, but at that time, Kiev lay in ruins, so he, as his predecessor had done, transferred the see to Vladimir.

At the very beginning of his service, Bishop Peter was obliged to bear an extremely heavy sorrow: certain people in the north of the country were dissatisfied with the selection of an abbot from the south of Russia to be metropolitan, and they made serious accusations against him. The affair was finally settled at a church council and concluded with the full vindication of the new metropolitan, whereas his opponents were disgraced. But Bishop Peter dealt with his opponents with such love that he immediately earned universal respect.

Meek and mild in matters that affected him personally, Bishop Peter was strict in his government of the Church. For the good of his flock, he traveled widely throughout Russia; he visited the Golden Horde, where he gained certain privileges for the clergy. In his time, Islam had begun to spread among the heathen Tatars; Khan Uzbek himself had become a Moslem. One of the preachers of Islam who called himself *Seidom* (which means a descendant of Mohammed) appeared among the Russians. Bishop Peter personally spoke against him and overcame him by the power of his words.

What saddened the bishop most of all were the dissensions among the Russian princes. He tried in every way possible to pacify them. On one occasion, he traveled for such purposes to Bryansk and was nearly killed for his efforts. The most serious of all these disagreements was the quarrel between the Grand Duke Mikhail Yaroslavitch of Tver (commemorated on November 22) and his nephew Prince Georgii Daniilovitch of Moscow. As a result of the latter's intrigues, the Grand Duke was stripped of his title and killed.

The bishop foresaw, however, that Moscow would unify Russia. He often visited this small and then unimportant town. The local prince, Georgii Daniilovitch, was constantly absent from his territory and entrusted the government to his brother, Prince John. Because of this prince's love for the poor, the people gave him the name *Kalita*, which comes from the word for a small leather money pouch. Metropolitan Peter was extremely close with Prince John and often conversed with him about Church affairs and the future of Moscow; he foretold the future greatness of the prince's family. The metropolitan wanted to transfer his see to Moscow where Prince John had built him a residence for his occasional visits, but before this could be done, it was necessary to construct a cathedral church. And so in 1326, in accordance with the metropolitan's plans, the construction of the Cathedral of the Dormition in the Moscow Kremlin was begun. In the foundations, near the altar, the bishop built himself a tomb.

After this, in a dream, the prince saw an extraordinarily high mountain covered with snow. The snow quickly melted, and then the mountain itself collapsed. The bishop interpreted the dream for the prince: the melting snow foretold his approaching death, and the mountain stood for the prince himself. The bishop received a revelation from on high about his own fast-approaching end, but it is not known in what manner he learned of this.

Soon after this, he died as he prayed at the hour of Vespers on December 21, 1326. The prince was away from the city at the time. When he returned, the body of the bishop was carried by priests to the Dormition Cathedral and buried there in the presence of an enormous crowd of people. During the funeral procession, a non-Orthodox Christian in the crowd saw the bishop seated in his coffin, blessing the throng on either side. Miracles of healing began from that moment.

Within a year, the Dormition Cathedral was completed and consecrated. Theognost, the new metropolitan, was faithful in all things to the memory and legacy of his departed predecessor. He continued to reside in

Moscow, constantly going to pray at the tomb of Bishop Peter and witnessing miracles. He informed the Patriarch of Constantinople about all this and received instructions to include this newly-appeared wonderworker in the company of the saints. The relics of St. Peter were discovered incorrupt three times: in 1382, during the attack by the Khan Tokhtamysh after the coffin was damaged by fire; in 1477, when the walls of the cathedral were pulled down; and in 1479, when the Dormition Cathedral was rebuilt in its present form by the Italian architect Fioravante.

Two discourses of St. Peter to his flock have survived, both dealing with the subject of family life. A *Life of St. Peter* was written by Prochorus, Bishop of Rostov, who was consecrated bishop by St. Peter himself, and another by Metropolitan Cyprian. His feast is kept on December 21 and on August 24.

English translation by Thomas Drain.

5. A Letter from Epiphanius the Wise to Cyril of Tver

Regarding the church of the *Sophia* (Holy Wisdom) in Constantinople, depicted in my book of the Gospel, called *Tetroevangelion* in Greek, which means a fourfold Gospel in our Russian tongue, this is how it came to be painted in my book. At that time, I lived in Moscow, where there dwelt a man, a famous sage, a very clever philosopher, Theophanes, a Greek, an eminent book-artist, and a fine painter among iconographers. He painted with his hand many different churches, more than forty of them: in Constantinople, in Chalcedon, in Galata, in Kapha, in Great Novgorod, and in Nizhni-Novgorod. Even in Moscow, there are three churches painted by him: the Annunciation of the Most Holy Mother of God, St. Michael's, and one more. In St. Michael's, he painted a city on the wall, with colors and in detail; on a stone wall at Prince Vladimir Andreevich's, he also painted Moscow itself. The palace of the great prince is painted in an unfamiliar but wonderful style. In the stone church of the Holy Annunciation, he also painted the Tree of Jesse and the Apocalypse. When he drew or painted these, no one ever saw him look at models anywhere, which some of our iconographers sometimes do, because they are filled with doubt in their continual perusal of their models, casting their eyes hither and thither. Theophanes, however, while drawing and painting with his hands, restlessly paced with his feet, talking in conversation with visitors with his tongue, while with his mind he contemplated things afar off and spiritual. With his spiritual eyes, he truly saw spiritual beauty. This admired and renowned man had a great love for my unworthiness, and so I, lowly and ignorant, gained much boldness before him. I often came for conversation with him since I always loved to talk with him.

Anyone who has a conversation with him, whether a short one or a long, can only wonder at his understanding, at his opinions, at his quick mind. I, seeing that he loved me and was not offended by my presence, added shamelessness to my boldness, and asked him the following:

I beg you, Lover of Wisdom, to paint for me a depiction of that great church of Holy Sophia which is in Constantinople, which the great Caesar Justinian erected, after taking an oath and likening himself to Solomon most wise. The quality and magnitude of this church is said by some to be like the Moscow Kremlin of the Inner City, with regards to the perimeter of the church and its foundation, and the time it takes to walk around it. If a stranger enters and wants to visit without a guide, he cannot come out without going astray, even if he consider himself very wise, because of the great multitude of columns and ways around them, of descents and ascents, passages and hallways, and sundry rooms, and chapels, and stairs and vestries, and crypts, and various partitions, and walls, and windows, and walks and doors, and entrances, and exits, and stone columns. Would you please paint for me the said Justinian, sitting on a horse, and holding a copper apple in his right hand, the size and the measure of which are reported sufficient to hold two and a half buckets of water. Would you also paint all the aforesaid on a page of a book so that I might place it at the beginning of my book. As long as I remember your painting and behold such a church, I shall imagine myself standing in Constantinople.

Being wise, he answered me wisely:

It is not possible either for you to obtain this or for me to paint it. Because of your insistence, however, I shall paint for you a small part of a fraction, and not merely of a fraction but of a hundredth part, to wit, a little out of much. Then, from this insignificant image painted by me, you may imagine and comprehend the immensity of the rest.

Having said this, he energetically took a brush and a sheet, quickly painted for me an image of a church along the lines of the church in Constantinople, and gave it to me. This sheet was also very useful to other Moscow iconographers, since there were many who copied it for themselves, competing with one another to get it and passing all around. After all of these, I got the drawing and used it to paint four images. I inserted the image of a church at four places in my book: 1) at the beginning of the book, in Matthew's Gospel, where I put Justinian's column and an image of the Evangelist Matthew, 2) before the evangelist Mark, 3) before the evangelist Luke, 4) at the beginning of John's Gospel. I painted four churches and four evangelists, which you saw once when I fled to Tver, fearful of an attack by Edigei, the emir of the Golden Horde (1408-1409), and found rest with you from my great tribulations, and I apprised you of my sorrow and showed you all my books which had remained with me after scattering and losses. It was then that you saw that church as I had painted it, and after six years, you reminded me of it this last winter by your kindness. So much for this. Amen.

English translation by Luben Stoilov

6. The Life of the Venerable Saint Andrei Rublev

[Please note that the numbers in parentheses indicate the works in the bibliography at the end of this section.]

The sources for the life of St. Andrei Rublev are very few. There is the *Life* of the venerable St. Nikon in two versions, long and short (1, page 138); the "Reply to those who love shameful things" of St. Joseph of Volokolomsk (2); a late 16th-century and early 17th-century document entitled *Account of the Holy Iconographers* (3, pp. 379-380); mention of him in the Russian Chronicles (4, p. 206-225); an early 19th-century transcription of the inscription on the grave of St. Andrei (5, p. 57); commemorations entered into the feast calendars (5, pp. 35-48).

The information given in the above accounts consists, for the most part, of brief separate entries of a general character. There is no independent *Life* of the saint although recognition of his holiness in these texts is unmistakable.

His work—portable panel icons and frescoes which he painted—provides an important addition to the few written sources for his life. In accord with the famous decision of the Seventh Ecumenical Council, the Orthodox Church honors the image as "equal with the Cross and the Gospel." Therefore, the making of images constitutes an exercise of piety which presupposes the assistance of grace from on high. An exercise of piety can develop into true holiness. For this reason, a special category in the Orthodox hierarchy of holiness, a special rank, is recognized for holy iconographers.

The first of the recognized iconographers is the holy apostle and evangelist Luke who, according to tradition, painted the first image of the Mother of God. In the Russian Church, St. Alipy of the Kiev Caves Monastery and St. Dionysius of Glushitsa are included among the iconographer saints. The most important of the Russian iconographers, however, is St. Andrei Rublev.

His principal works are the following:

1) the icon screen and the frescoes of the Cathedral of the Annunciation in the Moscow Kremlin (1405);

2) the frescoes and the icon screen in the Cathedral of the Dormition in Vladimir (1408);

3) the icon of our Lady of Vladimir for the Cathedral of the Dormition in Vladimir;

4) the frescoes and the icon screen in the Cathedral of the Dormition in Zvenigorod (end of the 14th-the beginning of the 15th centuries);

5) the Deisis row of the icon screen from the Cathedral of the Nativity of the Mother of God in the Monastery of St. Sava of Storozhevsk (beginning of the 15th century);

6) the frescoes and the icon screen of the Trinity Cathedral in the Holy Trinity-St. Sergius Monastery (painted between 1420-1430);

7) the icon of the Holy Trinity from that Cathedral;

8) the frescoes in the Cathedral of the Savior in the Andronikov Monastery in Moscow (early twenties of the 15th century).

The majority of these works were executed together with other master painters. All these images, however, produced in a spirit of Christian brotherhood, unity, and asceticism bear the unmistakable mark of holiness which we attribute above all to St. Andrei, in accordance with what we know of him and his fellow ascetics.

The most outstanding of his works is the icon of the Holy Trinity which, in the unanimous opinion of specialists, was painted by St. Andrei himself.

St. Andrei doubtless executed more frescoes and icons than those mentioned above, but written documentation of his other works has not been preserved.

Historical evidence about St. Andrei is meager in the extreme. Nothing is known of his origins. Some light might be shed on this subject by the existence of the second name, "Rublev," which remained attached to him even after he had become a monk. Apparently "Rublev" was a sort of birth name, that is, a family name. It has the characteristic ending of a Russian family name. In the 14th-15th centuries—in the period when the venerable St. Andrei lived—and for a considerable period afterwards, only members of the highest ranks of society bore family names (6, 167-169), a fact that further supports the theory that he was born in educated circles.

In addition, the sources point out his unusual skill, to which his work bears witness.

We do not know the year of the venerable St. Andrei's birth. It has been proposed that he was born about 1360. This year has now become a conventional date accepted by contemporary historians. If we presume that he was a relatively young man in 1405 when his name is first mentioned in the *Chronicles*, his date of birth can be advanced to the seventies or eighties of the 14th century. In the list of names given in the *Chronicles*, his name appears in the last (third) place, and it follows that he was the youngest of the master painters. He began to study his art from earliest childhood, and he very quickly arrived at a professional level. The exceptionally high quality of St. Andrei's work and the deep and moving sincerity in the spiritual content of his painting are especially characteristic of him; they cause us to ask the question of where St. Andrei studied the art of painting.

At the present time, it has become possible to consider that during the early period of his life St. Andrei studied and worked in Byzantium and Bulgaria. It is well-known that many Russians traveled in the Balkans, to Mount Athos, to Constantinople and to the Holy Land and not infrequently remained in those places for more or less extended periods. Thus, Athanasius Vyssotski, the disciple of St. Sergius of Radonezh, and doubtless known personally to St. Andrei, spent more than twenty full years in Constantinople working with a group of other monks on the translation and transcription of the works of Church Fathers. In Constantinople, there were even icons of the Russian saints—among them the icon of Ss. Boris and Gleb. Such icons were also specially painted to fill commissions from the Russian Church; thus, the aforementioned Athanasius Vyssotski obtained for Russia the renowned Vyssotski Chin—the set of icons of the Deisis painted for the Serpukhov Vyssotski Monastery which he had founded. All the specialists are agreed that St. Andrei must have been familiar with those icons. It is known that iconographers accompanied ambassadors sent from Russia to Constantinople.

Part of St. Andrei's artistic legacy consists of the depiction of a Greek sailing ship in the fresco *The Earth and the Sea Give up Their Dead* in the Dormition Cathedral, Vladimir, dated 1408. The masts, yards, hull, and flag on the stern are all depicted with a lively understanding of ship construction; it is difficult to believe that anyone could have acquired such knowledge in land-locked Russia. Two conclusions are possible: either 1) St. Andrei himself saw such ships, that is, he traveled by sea or 2) he learned about these details from his teacher, an artist of Greek origin. According to the second hypothesis, St. Andrei was the student of the renowned Theophanes the Greek. This theory is based on the fact that in a chronicle dated 1405, their names are mentioned together, Theophanes being mentioned first. That Theophanes was a definite and perhaps even a major influence on St.

Andrei can be considered beyond any doubt because they worked together for a certain time, and the younger Andrei, naturally, noted with great care how the renowned Greek worked. There is, however, no evidence of any closer collaboration. On the contrary, the fact that the 1405 chronicle also mentions along with them another master—the elder Prokhor from Gorodets, who had no association with Theophanes—should rather be considered as evidence of the absence of any close contacts between Theophanes and St. Andrei. For all that, it is certain that St. Andrei was a man thoroughly steeped in the culture of his time. In addition, the ascetic quality of St. Andrei's life, on the one hand, and the very character of Theophanes, on the other, speak more against the possibility of their having worked together in a systematic way. St. Andrei could have received a religious formation which would have enabled him to penetrate the spiritual depths of appearances only in a milieu where such studies were cultivated—above all in Byzantium. Therefore, the hypothesis that postulates a Greek education for St. Andrei is not without foundation.

St. Andrei lived in a period of major historical events. He was a witness to, and perhaps a participant in, these events which often turned out badly for Russia. In 1380, the bloody battlefield of Kulikovo took place, an event which marked the beginning of the liberation of Russia from the Tartar yoke. Two years later, Moscow was attacked and burned by Tokhtamysh. It is entirely probable that these and other similar shocks influenced St. Andrei's choice of the monastic life.

In 1395, Russia suffered another invasion; this time it was Tamerlane's horde that swept over the country. Even disregarding the preparedness of Grand Duke Vassily Dmitrievich to repel the invasion, his chances of victory were very small, given the colossal number of the enemy. The only remaining hope lay in the protection of the

Mother of God. The wonder-working icon of our Lady of Vladimir was transferred from Vladimir to Moscow. The entire population, with Metropolitan Cyprian at its head, went out to meet the holy icon at the spot where later, after the event, a monastery was founded, named the Monastery of the Holy Meeting.

The Church called everyone to prayer, fasting, and repentance. A miracle occurred: the Mother of God appeared in a dream to Tamerlane (Temir Aksaky) and sternly forbade him to march on Moscow. Proceeding to the Yelets, Tamerlane turned back and disappeared as quickly as he had appeared. Soon thereafter, St. Andrei painted a copy of the icon of the Vladimir Mother of God with the blessing of Metropolitan Cyprian.

It is not known for certain where St. Andrei was tonsured a monk, but throughout his life, he was associated with two monasteries: 1) the Holy Trinity-St. Sergius Monastery outside Moscow and 2) the Spasso-Andronikov Monastery in the city itself. A tradition, which dates from the end of the 16th century, sees in St. Andrei a spiritual son of the venerable St. Nikon of Radonezh. Contemporary research, however, shows that most probably he made his monastic profession in the Spasso-Andronikov Monastery (5, p. 40-43). These two versions do not substantially contradict one another since both monasteries were very closely associated. St. Andrei was apparently under obedience to St. Nikon when he worked in the Trinity Monastery, and naturally this was remembered. Insofar as the monk Andrei constantly filled commissions from the metropolitan and the grand duke, it would be natural for him to be, as the saying goes, "at hand," that is, in one of Moscow's religious communities, namely, the Spasso-Andronikov Monastery. It is possible, as well, that St. Andrei had some earlier connection with the St. Sergius Monastery which is unknown to us. In any case St. Andrei was in spirit undoubtedly a disciple of St. Sergius.

Even if he resided at the Andronikov Monastery, the monk Andrei lived in the milieu of St. Sergius' disciples, with whom he was closely linked when he traveled while fulfilling painting commissions. In addition to St. Nikon, he apparently also knew St. Sava of Storozkevsk since he worked at the turn of the 14th-15th centuries in Zvenigorod and shortly thereafter at the Savvino-Storozhevsk Monastery itself. He would also have known St. Sergius' nephew, St. Theodore, archbishop of Rostov, who for a while was the abbot of the Simonov Monastery, the neighbor of the Andronikov Monastery. Another abbot of that monastery, and an associate of St. Sergius, St. Cyril, in 1392 left for Belozersk, but as a personality he must have been known to the monk Andrei. Finally, St. Andronik, the founder and first abbot of the monastery that bears his name, was a prominent disciple of St. Sergius. The links with the Trinity-St. Sergius Monastery were constant and varied. A number of monks transferred from the Trinity Monastery to the Andronikov Monastery. Among them was Ermolai-Ephrem, a future abbot of the monastery, who contributed the funds to construct a stone church and with whom the monk Andrei had close ties (7, pp. 326-330). Doubtless St. Andrei also knew Epiphanius the Wise, known to be a disciple of St. Sergius, who wrote the first historical record of the Andronikov Monastery and left us the account of Theophanes the Greek. No mention of the monk Andrei appears in Epiphanius' writing; this is completely natural insofar as he was writing about the past and not dealing with contemporary events.

Living in such an advanced spiritual milieu, in an atmosphere of holiness, the monk Andrei was able to profit not only from historic precedents of sanctity but also from the living examples he saw in the ascetics who surrounded him. He immersed himself deeply in the teachings of the Church and in the lives of the saints whom he depicted, which pushed his talent toward artistic and spiritual perfection.

In addition to Epiphanius the Wise, the monk Andrei was well-acquainted with other highly educated men of his time, with whom he was in close contact. Among these, first mention should be given to Cyprian, the metropolitan of Moscow. The monk Andrei was very close to the spiritual world of Archbishop Cyprian, who had been schooled in Athonite monasticism. Andrei's contact with him was fairly close since they shared an interest in Athonite monasticism and St. Cyprian, who was accustomed to the intellectual atmosphere of Byzantium, surrounded himself with the most spiritual and best educated Russians in Moscow. This close contact meant that St. Andrei's spiritual genealogy goes back to the two sources of Athonite hesychasm, since Metropolitan Cyprian was a disciple of St. Philotheos the Patriarch, who was a disciple of Gregory Palamas, and a relative (as it is supposed) of St. Epithemius, the Patriarch of Tirnova, a disciple of St. Theodosius of Tirnova, who was himself a disciple of St. Gregory the Sinaite (8, pp 15, 19, 24). The sources for St. Andrei's life speak of the elevation "of the intellect and the understanding" to "the unsubstantial and divine light" accomplished by means of the contemplation of holy icons —"the elevation of the sense of sight." It is no accident that this absolutely hesychastic trait was attributed to both St. Andrei and his "companion in fasting," Daniel (2, columns 557-558). We might even go so far as to say that very few analogous instances can be found in Russian hagiography.

It is also certain that the monk Andrei was also closely acquainted with the Metropolitan St. Photius, who succeeded the deceased Metropolitan Cyprian in 1409. We can reach this conclusion with complete probability if only from the fact that in 1408 Andrei and

Daniel painted the frescoes in the metropolitan's cathedral in Vladimir in preparation for the arrival of Photius. Photius was another of those bishops who belonged to the circle of highly educated, spiritual and civil officials, and who produced a series of spiritual writings that the monk Andrei undoubtedly knew (8, p. 15).

"Surpassing all men in great knowledge," in the words of St. Joseph of Volokolamsk, the monk Andrei was well-acquainted with the writings of the holy fathers and teachers of the Church. He doubtless knew the writings of St. Dionysius the Areopagite which had been translated into Old Church Slavonic in the 14th century by the monk Isaiah at the command of the highest Church authorities in conjunction with the hesychastic controversies (8, pp. 14-16). He was also intimately acquainted with the writings of St. Gregory the Sinaite, which were by then available to the Russian reader. Other works in circulation among educated persons and, doubtless, known to St. Andrei, were the *Theology* of St. John of Damascus, the *Hexameron* of John the Exarch, the *Biblical Chronicle Explained*, and other works of Orthodox writers and Fathers of the Church.

In 1406, as the *Chronicle* informs us, St. Andrei and Daniel painted frescoes in the Dormition Cathedral in Vladimir. The following entry appears for that year in the *Chronicle*: "In that same year, on the 25th of May, the masters Daniel the monk and Andrei Rublev began to paint the great Cathedral of the Immaculate Lady of Vladimir, at the order of the grand duke."

In this short entry in the *Chronicle*, attention is directed to the date given for the beginning of the work of painting the church. This is an exceptional occurrence. Apparently, the work of frescoing the church was given an enormous significance, which is explained by the expected arrival from Constantinople of the new metropolitan, Photius, who succeeded to the see in 1409 after

Cyprian's death in 1406. Vladimir continued to be considered the city and residence of the metropolitan, and the great church there continued to be his cathedral. For this reason, the metropolitan cathedral had to have wall-paintings worthy of the high station of this representative of the Church of Constantinople, and had to show at the same time the dignity of the Russian Church. In this way, the iconographers were fulfilling in their own fashion a "mission of representation" whose task was especially difficult, if we take into account the exceptionally high demands on sacred art made by the Greek Church at that time. These demands required, in the first place, that art witness to Truth and that the quality of the work be judged on this basis. In this regard, the new metropolitan was undoubtedly well-acquainted with and competent to judge ecclesiastical art, which follows from his Constantinopolitan education.

This high mission was entrusted to Daniel the Black and St. Andrei, who is mentioned in second place, as the younger of the two. These iconographers worthily fulfilled the assignment given them.

The monk Andrei was mentioned in 1408 for the first time together with his "fellow ascetic," Daniel the Black also living an advanced spiritual life. From this year on, we know about the close spiritual bond between two ascetic iconographers, a bond which continued for about twenty years until their deaths. The beautiful, if brief, testimony about the spirit of Christian love which united them presents us with the highest example of that love, similar to the examples which we find in the tales of the early ascetics of the Christian East. The tradition regarding the close spiritual bond between St. Andrei and Daniel was carefully preserved through the 15th century and was committed to writing by St. Joseph of Volokolamsk, in the words of the former abbot of the Trinity-St. Sergius Monastery, Spiridon. We give here the widely-known text:

> ... and this honorable elder Spiridon told us
> about the wonderful and excellent iconographers
> Daniel and his disciple Andrei . . . . They performed
> many good deeds and were very observant of the life
> of fasting and of the monastic life. They both were
> filled with divine grace and arrived at such a state of
> divine love that they were never concerned with
> earthly things, but always had their minds and
> thoughts lifted on high to the uncreated and divine
> light, while their bodily eyes were ever fixed on the
> colors of things, on the painted images of Christ the
> Master, of his most Pure Mother, and of all the saints.
> And on the feast of the glorious Resurrection, they
> both sat on seats, and they placed before them the
> most pure and divine icons, gazing at them con-
> stantly, being filled with divine joy and light. So nei-
> ther on that day nor on any other day when the work
> of painting was forbidden, did they do any work. For
> these reasons, Christ the Master glorified them at
> their last hour: Andrei died first, and then his fellow
> ascetic Daniel took sick, and in his last moments of
> life, he saw Andrei in great glory calling him to eter-
> nal and endless beatitude (2, column 557).

This short account transmitted by St. Joseph gives us
a wonderfully bright image of the two ascetic artists—
true monks and true ascetics. They "arrived" at that divine Love which was revealed to them and attracted
them to Himself.

This short entry of St. Joseph gives us a surprisingly
clear image of these two spiritual witnesses: iconographers, true monks and ascetics. They succeeded in "win-
ning" the love of God which opened up to them and
which welcomed them. St. Joseph explains their complete abandonment of any earthly consideration in order
to conquer this divine grace. They "were never concerned
with earthly things." We have already noted before their

deepened hesychastic experience. St. Joseph made a succinct presentation of their experience and their attitude
in relation to iconography which represents a complete
spiritual experience and which teaches us how to receive
icons correctly. The contemplation of icons was for them
a feast that filled their hearts "with divine joy and light"
to the degree that it raised their spirits beyond the colors
and the "material archetypes."

This contemplation allowed them to rise above mere,
immobile material imitation to the immaterial Arche-
type who gives life to the world. Here is the exceptional
importance of the icon as a witness to the truth. From
this approach, we can see that each brush stroke is specially inspired. It is "for these reasons," that is, for a life-
style both elevated and spiritual, that "Christ the Master
glorified them at their last hour." After the death of St.
Andrei, "his fellow ascetic," Daniel, who had not been
separated from him in heart until death, received on his
deathbed the news of the glorification of his spiritual
brother in the kingdom of heaven: "Daniel ... saw
Andrei in glory calling him to eternal and endless beati-
tude." This very important piece of testimony is also reported in another version in *The Life and Works of St.
Nikon of Radonezh*, contained in the chronicle written by
Pachomius the Logothete: "As soon as Daniel arrived at
the moment of leaving this material world, he saw his beloved friend who called him to come join him in a life of
great happiness. When Daniel perceived Andrei expressing his desire, he was filled with joy and told the vision of
his friend to the other monks present. Then he died" (10,
pp. 2905-2906).

We therefore have two indications dealing with the
posthumous glory of St. Andrei. Even though Andrei was
younger than Daniel in this world, he appeared as his elder in the spiritual world, and, in a certain way, it was
Andrei who received soul of Daniel, the Righteous one,

at the moment when his soul left his body. Therefore, the final resting place of the two heroes in the faith is the Spasso-Andronikov Monastery.

The memory of the two iconographers, especially that of St. Andrei, was the object of great veneration all through the 16th and 17th centuries. In the middle of the 16th century, the Council of One Hundred Chapters decreed that the future St. Andrei Rublev should serve as the universal model for all other iconographers and that the icon of the Holy Trinity should be painted henceforth according to the model of Andrei Rublev and "the famous Greek artists."

By this action, St. Andrei was recognized as the equal of the "famous" Byzantine artists, most of whom were in reality unknown, but who at the time fixed the canons of Orthodox iconography. It is quite possible that the model of an iconographer, sketched in section 43 of the Council of One Hundred Chapters and widely diffused in the pattern books, was in large measure inspired by the tradition dealing with St. Andrei since he was well-known to the Fathers of this council.

We find a witness to the holiness of the venerable Andrei in the original Stroganov pattern book of the end of the 16th century. It seems that this original pattern book was composed in the circle of court iconographers and that it had a great influence and considerable authority. The manual has this to say: "The venerable Andrei de Radonezh, iconographer, surnamed Rublev, painted many holy icons, all miraculous ... He had formerly lived in obedience to the venerable Nikon of Radonezh who ordered the icon of the Holy Trinity to be painted in his presence, to the glory of his spiritual father St. Sergius the Wonderworker ... " (3, pp. 379-380). In this text, St. Andrei is called "venerable," as well as Daniel some pages later. All his icons were recognized as great sources of grace, and it is noted that Andrei followed in the spiritual tradition of Ss. Sergius and Nikon. The name of St. Andrei, along with that of Daniel, are also found in ancient liturgical calendars.

Until the 17th century, the place of their burial was known. According to a later source, "their holy relics were buried in the Spasso-Andronikov Monastery, under the old bell tower, which was destroyed recently and whose area was leveled so that all kinds of impure people now trample on it. The memory of these relics has thus been forgotten" (5, p. 47). The ancient bell tower used to be, so it is thought, northwest of the western part of the Cathedral of the Holy Savior. The only way to be sure of its exact location is to carry out archeological excavations.

In small drawings contained in some 16th-century manuscripts, St. Andrei is represented with a halo: see the chronicler Ostermanovski, the life and works of St. Sergius represented in portraits, end of the 15th century, in the ancient collection of the library of the Trinity-St. Sergius Monastery.

The sources thus mentioned attest that from the 15th to the 17th centuries, no one doubted the holiness of Andrei Rublev, nor the eminent spiritual heights of Daniel. According to the tradition of the Trinity-St. Sergius Monastery, St. Andrei Rublev's feast day was on July 4, the feast day of St. Andrew of Crete (11, p. 109).

During the 18th and 19th centuries, however, many Orthodox traditions were forgotten, especially those relating to canonical iconography. This period was therefore not a good one for remembering and venerating the holy iconographers. The reputation of St. Andrei Rublev was not reborn until the beginning of the 20th century when an interest in the traditions of Orthodox iconography was also reborn. Throughout the 20th century, the veneration of St. Andrei's memory has grown in an extraordinary way ... We cannot help seeing here a manifestation of God's will, for especially in the 20th century, St. Andrei's icon of the Holy Trinity, as well as his other works, have become witnesses for true Orthodoxy to the whole world.

The venerable Andrei was glorified on the basis of the holiness of his life, of his spiritual deeds as an iconographer, and of his witnessing, like that of an evangelist, a witnessing that continues today to teach people the truth without lies about God worshipped in the Trinity; his sanctity is also based on the testimony to his holiness contained in the writings of the venerable Joseph of Volokolamsk.

Bibliography of Russian Texts

1. PSRL (The Complete Collection of Russian Chronicles), vol. VI.

2. *Velikiye Minyei-Chet'i* (The Lives of the Saints) September 9.

3. Buslayev, F. I., *Istoricheskiye ochyerki russkoi narodnoi slovestnosti i iskusstva* (Historical Studies of Russian Folk Literature and Art) Volume 2, 1861.

4. Tikhomirov, M. N., "Andrei Rublev i evo epokha (Andrei Rublev and His Epoch) in *Russkaya kultura XI-XVIII vyekov* (Russian Culture from the Eleventh to the Eighteenth Century), Moscow, 1968.

5. Bryusova, V. G., "Spornye voprosy biografii Andreya Rubleva" (Disputed Questions about the Biography of Andrei Rublev) in *Voprosy Istorii,* vol. 1, 1969.

6. Nikonov, V. A., *Imya i Obshchestvo* (Name and Society), Moscow, 1974.

7. Voronin, N. N., *Zodchestvo severo-vostochnoi Rusi XII-XV vekov* (The Architecture of Northeastern Russia from the Twelfth to the Fifteenth Century), vol. II, Moscow, 1962.

8. Saltykov, A. A., "O znacheniyi areopagitik v dryevnyerusskom iskusstvye (kings izucheniyu 'Troitsy' Andreya Rubleva) (The Significance of the Areopagite in Old Russian Art [with reference to the *Trinity* of Andrei Rublev]) in *Drevnyerusskoye Iskusstvo XV-XVII*

vekov, Moscow, 1981.

9. "Poslaniye Epifaniya Premudrovo Kirillu Tverskomu" (The Letter of Epiphanius the Wise to Cyril of Tver) in Vzdornov, G. I., *Feofan Grek. Tvorcheskoye Naslediye* (Feofan the Greek. The Artistic Heritage), Moscow, 1983.

10. *Vyelikiye Minyei-Chet'yi* (The Lives of the Saints), November.

11. Sergeyev, V.N., *Rublev,* Moscow, 1986.

12. PSRL, vol. XVIII.

English translation by Thomas Drain.

7. Saint Dionysius of Glushitsa

A certain native of Vologda came to the Spasso-Kamennii Monastery on Lake Kubensk when the abbot was Dionysius the Hagiorite (commemorated on October 23) and was tonsured a monk with the name Dionysius. This monk Dionysius, after living there for nine years practicing monastic asceticism, received the blessing of the superior of the community to set out—with his fellow ascetic, a monk named Pachomius—for a remote and deserted place called St. Luke's, since at one time there had been a monastery there dedicated to St. Luke the Evangelist. The hermits erected a church dedicated to St. Nicholas and then, leaving the elder Pachomius in charge, St. Dionysius set out farther into the dense forest of Vologda, and toward evening of that day, he stopped for the night on the banks of the river Glushitsa. As he slept, he heard a peal of bells and understood that this was meant as a sign from the Lord himself to build a monastery on that spot. He built himself a cell, a lean-to, which rested against the trunk of a bird-cherry tree, and fed himself from the berries of that tree. Later, he gave these berries to the sick who came to visit him, and they were healed. And, until our own day, these berries have retained their healing power. St. Dionysius settled on the Glushitsa in the year 1393. When disciples began to gather around him, the local prince sent woodsmen to clear land for the construction of a monastery. The brethren erected a small wooden church dedicated to the Protection of the Most Holy Mother of God, together with some cells for the monks. The brotherhood grew quickly. Once, after long prayer, St. Dionysius fell asleep. While he slept, he saw a handsome young man who commanded him to construct a bigger church. In the dream, as he did so, the young man said, "You have as your protector and helper the Most Holy Mother of God, from now and forever." The saint awoke, and from that moment, he was not able go back to sleep. After matins, he told the brethren about his dream, concluding his account with these words: "Our duty is to fulfill this command, calling on the help of the Lord and his Most Pure Mother, for she will assist us!" The church was built and decorated with icons painted by St. Dionysius, for he was a talented icon-painter and could do anything with his hands, from forging iron to sewing clothing. Thus the foundations were laid for the great Glushitsa Lavra. This was in the year 1407. The local prince, George Bokhtyuzhskii, expressed the desire to contribute funds for the foundation of the monastery, but the saint would not accept the money. Considering the ardor of the prince's faith and his zeal, St. Dionysius did agree that he could provide food for the brethren.

When the lavra had become crowded with monks, St. Dionysius found an isolated spot of which he was very fond. It was on the banks of the Glushitsa and was called Sosnovyets, from a gigantic centuries-old pine tree that grew in the swampy ground in that area. There St. Dionysius constructed a church dedicated to the Holy Forerunner of the Lord, St. John the Baptist, and a few monastic cells for some brethren who, like himself, loved to live in the wilderness and had accompanied him in his move. Once settled there, he intensified his ascetic practices, taking for his nourishment only bread and water, and passing every night standing in prayer. There he dug his own grave over which he often prayed. He frequently passed entire nights in prayer, oblivious of the freezing temperatures. To the brethren, he often spoke thus:

> If my body is not laid to rest here, then do not remain here, for this is a deserted and difficult place. But if I am buried here, then for goodness' sake, do not despise this place and me, for those who continue to live here will receive their reward from God, and on the fearful day of judgment will find for themselves a helper in our Lady, for they have struggled in this monastery.

And so it came to pass. The lavra was abandoned, but the Sosnovyets Monastery continued to be occupied until very recent times.

St. Dionysius founded five men's monasteries and one named for St. Leontius of Rostov for his women disciples; he directed them all. Twice he visited his abba, Dionysius, the archbishop of Rostov, formerly the abbot of the Spasso-Kemennii Monastery, in whose diocese the territory of Vologda was located. The holy bishop blessed him with an icon of the Mother of God and furnished the monastery churches with the things necessary to celebrate the liturgy. Among the disciples of St. Dionysius, who were renowned for the holiness of their lives, were the venerable saints Macarius, Amphilochius, and Tarasius (commemorated on October 12), Gregory of Pel'shma (commemorated on September 30), and Philip Rabangskii (commemorated on November 14). The venerable St. Stephen of Komelsk (commemorated on June 12) came to the lavra after the death of St. Dionysius.

The saint always taught his disciples to call nothing their own, to pray constantly, and to keep in mind the hour of their death. But above all else, he taught them obedience. The saint ordered one monk, who had caught a large number of fish without the blessing of the superior, to throw out the fish he had caught, saying, "If you sow with a blessing, you will reap a blessing; God desires obedience and not sacrifices." Another monk who had died was found to have been in possession of a few coins; the saint ordered the money to be thrown out, together with the body of the disobedient monk, and he did not immediately give his blessing for his burial so that through fear all insubordination would be eliminated from the monastery. St. Dionysius' main virtue was his charity and love of the brothers. During a famine, a large number of the needy came; and the more people came, the more mercifully the saint dipped into the monastery reserves. Finally, the cellarer came to him and said that the reserves of the monastery were no longer sufficient for such charity. But the saint countered his statement with these words:

> Remember the words of the Savior: "Do not be anxious about tomorrow, for your heavenly Father knows that you need all these things. But seek first the Kingdom of Heaven and all these things shall be added to you." (Matt. 6: 31-33) "Be merciful as your Heavenly Father is merciful." For about no other sin but mercilessness do we hear our gentle God pronounce judgment with such anger: "Depart from me you cursed into the eternal fire prepared for the devil and his angels." (Matt. 25: 41) "For judgment is without mercy to one who has shown no mercy." (Jas. 2:13) Let us flee from mercilessness and idleness to good works, for nothing can help us like mercy, and God will return the measure with which the merciful man measures his assistance to the needy, according to the promise of the Holy Scriptures.

Thieves once stole the monastery horses. Informed of the theft, St. Dionysius said with a smile, "If I had found the thieves, I would have added something else from our possessions, and looked after them with love."

But for the thieves, the affair came to an unhappy end. They stopped to rest in a field where grain was being dried; suddenly the grain caught fire. The thieves were barely able to save their lives by fleeing, but the horses burned to death. Seeing the life of St. Dionysius, which was so pleasing to God, the devils wreaked their malice on him. While he was still living at Glushitsa, they once threw him under the floor and weighed him down with a floorboard, so that his disciple Macarius found him barely breathing.

Foreseeing his approaching end, St. Dionysius chose as his successor his closest assistant, Amphilochius. He himself prayed constantly for the brethren to the Most Holy Mother of God. Once, after such a prayer, he heard a voice in his sleep: "Your prayer for the brethren has been heard, and without interruption, I will abide in this monastery, protecting it from every evil and need." When the saint awoke, his heart was trembling with joy. He revealed to Amphilochius what he had learned in the dream. On the 29th of May, his final illness began, during which it was revealed to him secretly that he would die in three days. On the last day, early in the morning, he gave his blessing to his close disciple, Macarius, to celebrate the Divine Liturgy so that he could receive Holy Communion for one last time, and then summoned the brethren himself for one final word of exhortation, during which he repeated his prophecy about the Sosnovyets Monastery: "If I find mercy with God," he concluded, "then I will not abandon this place, but I will pray for it to the Lord and his Most Pure Mother." His countenance shone with divine light. He blessed the brethren for the last time and quietly gave up his soul to God. The cell was filled with a wonderful fragrance, and at that very minute, Amphilocius saw a marvelous crown on his head. This took place on June 1, 1437, at six o'clock in the morning. St. Dionysius was 74 and a half years old.

He was buried at Sosnovyets, in accordance with his wishes. His body was carried to the grave on a mule. At one point, the mule stopped and refused to go farther. A chapel was later constructed on this spot. Then St. Amphilochius arranged for another mule, which St. Dionysius especially loved, to carry his master to his last resting-place. St. Amphilocius, his disciple and successor, was buried alongside him. A description of the physical appearance of St. Dionysius has survived: he was short of stature, thin, with a flowing beard down to his chest and with gentle eyes. His face was oval; his hair light brown, about half of it gray. In the Church of the Nativity in the Sosnovyets Monastery among other antiquities, two icons painted by St. Dionysius are preserved: one of the Mother of God Hodoguitria, the other of the Most Holy Mother of God of the Sign, with the fiery seraphim. The monastery also keeps a portion of the saint's staff.

English translation by Thomas Drain.

8. Saint Cornelius of the Pskov Caves

The holy and venerable martyr Cornelius was the son of Steven and Mary, boyars from Pskov. He received his education at the Spasso-Mirozhsky Monastery (the Savior of Mirozh), near Pskov. This monastery was well-known as a center of icon painting. It was there that the venerable Cornelius studied this art. In his early youth, he entered the small, poor Monastery of the Pskov Caves which had been founded in the 15th century on the spot where the hermit Mark had carried out his ascetical exploits. The monastery is not far from Pskov, in the middle of hills covered with a deep virgin forest. At 28, Cornelius became the hegumen of the monastery. By his strict personal life and his wise administration, he was able to raise his monastery to a high degree of spirituality, assembling around him more than 100 monks. He sent those novices who showed artistic talent to the Spasso-Mirozhsky Monastery to learn to paint icons while he himself painted a great number of icons for his monastery. He painted one miraculous icon of the Mother of God called the Pechersky Icon of Tenderness. The monastery was surrounded by high walls and became an impregnable fortress which withstood Steven Bathory's siege of in 1581 and maintained its importance up to the time of Peter the Great when the Russians established themselves in the Baltic region. The intellectual elite of Russia greatly honored the venerable Cornelius and loved to gather at the monastery. Among them was Muromtzeff, a friend of Prince Andre Kurbsky, who became a monk with the name of Bassian. Moreover, when Kurbsky committed treason and went over to the Lithuanians, the venerable Cornelius and Muromtzeff stopped writing to him altogether. The venerable Cornelius wrote the annals of his monastery and other works which have not come down to us. There is some indication that in one of them, Cornelius denounced Ivan the Terrible's cruelty.

He also gave himself to missionary activity in the local population and helped the people very much during the war against the Teutonic knights. When the Russians had laid siege to Narva, some drunken Germans threw the icon of the Mother of God into the fire. In an instant, the fire roared up, a fire broke out, and the Russians took the city. As for the holy icon and the icon of St. Nicholas, they were found undamaged under the debris. The venerable Cornelius sent some holy water to those laying siege to the city of Fellin, and when it arrived, a fire broke out inside the walls. The Russians were thus able to capture the city. In 1570, Tsar Ivan the Terrible, having just destroyed Novgorod, arrived in Pskov. The venerable Cornelius was part of the group of priests who came out to greet him. The tsar spared the city, but when he arrived at the Monastery of the Pskov Caves, he beat the venerable Cornelius with his sceptre, very close to the holy doors. The monks removed Cornelius' body right away and carried it to the cave where they buried him. The road that leads from the holy doors to the cave, having been sprinkled with blood, is still called the "bloody road." Bassian, the disciple of Cornelius, was also killed. St. Cornelius was then 69 years old.

The saint's relics were put into an open reliquary. In 1581, during Steven Bathory's siege of Pskov, the monk Dorotheus saw the venerable Anthony of the Kievan Caves in the air, the holy Prince Vladimir equal-to-the-apostles, the holy Prince Vsevolod and Dovmonta of Pskov, friends of God, and St. Nicholas Salos who prayed to the Mother of God in favor of the city under attack. Steven Bathory was forced to lift the siege and to retreat. The icon on which this event is represented is called the Icon of the Pskov Caves.

9. Saint Pimen of Zographou

The prominent iconographer and church builder, the venerable Pimen of Zographou, was born in Sofia. He was the blessed fruit of the long prayers of his parents. His mother had been blessed to see the Holy Theotokos in her dreams. She was dressed in white and surrounded by a large number of monks. The Holy Mother promised Pimen's mother that her barrenness would soon come to an end by the birth of a son. The child was born on the day of the princes of the apostles Peter and Paul (June 29) and received the baptismal name of Paul. His parents saw to it that he studied reading, writing, iconography, church chanting, and the Holy Scriptures. The child received his training from his parents' spiritual father, the hieromonk Thomas of the Zographou Monastery who was serving at that time in the ancient city church of the holy great Martyr George. After the death of his parents, the young Paul's teacher also died. On the 40th day after the teacher's death, Paul had a vision in which Fr. Thomas appeared to his disciple and advised him to go to Mount Athos where he would find his salvation. Paul gave the rest of his parents' property to the poor and went off to the Bulgarian Monastery of Zographou on Mount Athos. He was soon tonsured a monk with the name of Pimen. The young monk quickly progressed in the monastic virtues that the brothers started calling him "the young abbot." One time, some envious brothers threw Pimen's cloak into a fire, but instead of burning, it put the fire out. Ashamed of what they had done, the jealous brothers stopped bothering Pimen. When he turned 30, brother Pimen was ordained a priest, against his will, by the Macedonian bishop, Pamphily of Voden who was Bulgarian by nationality. The venerable Pimen always served covered in tears, crying profusely, and received from God the gift of miracle-working prayer: he healed one brother stricken with rabies and saved the life of another brother bitten by a poisonous snake.

In order to avoid becoming proud of the great respect which all the brothers were showing him, Pimen received the blessing of the monastery's hegumen to leave the monastery and devote himself to the simple life. He built a very simple shelter in the forest eating only chestnuts and different kinds of grass. He would come to the monastery only to receive Holy Communion. Once in the presence of two brothers from the monastery, a forest fire started and when it got close to the shelter of the venerable Pimen, he prayed for a torrential rain, which occurred right away, and the fire was put out.

When he was 55 years old, during prayer, the holy patron of the Zographou Monastery, the great martyr and victory bearer George told him that God's will for him was to be a pastor to his own nation which had been left without pastors. Because of his fear of being deceived, the venerable Pimen asked for advice from an elderly starets and only after receiving the old monk's agreement did Pimen go to Bulgaria which at that time suffering under the Turkish yoke. Pimen took with him his disciple Pamphily, who later on was to write Pimen's *Life.* Crying monastery brothers went with them to the outskirts of the Zographou Monastery. For many years, Pimen traveled through almost all of Bulgaria. First he was in his own city of Sofia and its surrounding area. After that, he went to southern Bulgaria and the Bachkovsky Monastery. He traveled all over northern Bulgaria visiting many towns like Silistra, Vidin, and others. Everywhere he preached God's word, strengthen and increased the faith of the Orthodox people. By his prayers, he performed many miracles, built and repaired many churches. In the Dorostol diocese, his prayers opened the eyes of a man born blind whom Pimen later on tonsured into monasticism, according to the man's own wish. He build and renovated about 300 churches and 15 monasteries, decorating them himself with frescoes. Among those are the Cherepish Monastery in the Vratza diocese and the Suhodal Monastery which at that time was in the Vidin diocese.

At the end of his life, the venerable Pimen went back to the Cherepish monastery to die. Soon he got very sick, gave to the monastery brothers his paternal blessing, took Holy Communion, and died on November 3, 1620. Before his death, his face shone and around his grave, many miracles took place. Some time later, Turkish bandits burned down the Cherepish Monastery and escaped into the wilderness. Then, the monks from the Suhodal Monastery opened the grave and moved the relics of the venerable Pimen to their monastery where they are to this day. This monastery once belonged to the Bulgarian diocese of Vidin, but now it is in Yugoslavia, in the Knyazhevats region. It is not know when saint Pimen of Zographou was canonized.

10. Saint Anastasius the New Martyr of Neapolis

St. Anastasius was born in Neapolis where he became a well-known painter. He became engaged to a young girl from a Christian family, but he soon broke off the engagement when he learned of her loose morals. In order to wreak vengeance, the girl's parents cast an evil spell on Anastasius which caused him to lose his reason. Thinking that he was "mad," the Turks succeeded in converting him. God took pity on him, however, and he soon recovered his health. When he came to his senses, he discovered that he had been circumcised and that he was wearing a Moslem turban. He then threw it down on the ground crying: "I was a Christian; I am and will always be a Christian."

The Turks, seeing him repent of his conversion to Islam, seized him, beat him, and forcibly took him before a judge who tried to convince him to deny Christ. At first, the judge tried clever ruses, then threats, but St. Anastasius remained unshakable and courageously confess his faith: "I do not renounce my Lord Jesus Christ, the true God, but I believe in him and worship him as my Creator and Savior. As for your faith, I want nothing to do with it; I hate both you and your prophet."

When the judge heard these words, he condemned St. Anastasius to be beheaded, but the Turks at the trial did not wait for the sentence to be carried out. They jumped on him and dragged him out of the courtroom. Some beat him with sticks; others cut him with knives. In this way, St. Anastasius became perfect and received the martyr's crown. Now he is a jewel among the martyrs for the glory of the Father, the Son, and the Holy Spirit. Amen.

11. Saint Iorest, Metropolitan of Transylvania

The holy hierarch Iorest was the son of Transylvanian peasants. Loving Christ from his childhood, he became a monk at the Putna monastery under the name of Iorest. Then, following in the spiritual school of the monastery, he became an accomplished monk, and a skilled calligrapher-iconographer. What is more, he was very zealous in the service of the Church and in safe-guarding the Orthodox faith. Due to the purity of his heart, the hegumen had him ordained a priest, and the pious Iorest became a lighted flame among the fathers, accomplishing holy things by the fear of God and consoling the people by teaching appropriate Christian doctrines.

His monastery's reputation came to the ears of the prince of Moldavia, Basil Lupu. Ghenady, the metropolitan of Transylvania, had died in the fall of 1640, and the pious Iorest of Putna was elected father and primate of the Church of Transylvania, with God's blessing. After being consecrated bishop by the metropolitan of Valachia, the gentle hierarch Iorest mounted the metropolitan throne of Transylvania at Alba Iulia.

During the three years of his pontificate, the holy hierarch Iorest fought like a true confessor defending the Orthodox faith in the face of foreign, Calvinist teachings as well as against all the sly traps of the demons. Everywhere, he installed zealous priests, founded churches, visited villages, consoled and taught the faithful like a good shepherd of Christ's flock.

In 1643, the holy hierarch Iorest was thrown in prison because of his zeal for the true faith. He suffered many insults, attacks, and outrageous things. But he endured everything like a martyr, being ready to give his life for the defense of the Orthodox faith and the salvation of his flock. After nine months, the true pastor was freed and forced to pay a large sum of money. He came back to Moldavia in 1656-1657 and became the bishop of Husi, again admirably leading the Church of Christ and working for the salvation of his spiritual children. Then he put his soul into the hands of the great high priest, Jesus

Christ, and joined the choir of holy confessors. The Romanian Orthodox Church glorified him in 1955 and commemorates him on April 24.

12. Saint Joseph the New Martyr of Constantinople

Joseph became a monk in the monastery of St. Dionysius on Mount Athos and was placed under the direction of the hegumen Stephen and became well-known for his monastic virtues. Joseph's superior ordered him to accompany the monk Evdokimos to his execution as a martyr because having previously renounced Christ [by becoming Moslem], Evdokimos now had to purify himself of his sin by shedding his blood. Once again, however, he renounced Christ when faced with the tortures inflicted by the Turks and denounced his companion, Joseph, as the person responsible for his defection from the Islamic faith. St. Joseph was then seized and put in prison in Constantinople where he was tortured cruelly. He nonetheless remained firm in his faith in Christ receiving the martyr's crown by being hanged in 1819. This holy iconographer had painted the icon of the holy Archangels on the iconostasis of his monastery's main church.

13. Two Russian Documents about Holy Iconographers

A) An Account of the Iconographers[1]

[SAKHAROV: *An Account of the Iconographers* was edited from two lists: one was received from M. S. Peshekhonor and the other from Grigoriev. The two lists are joined together in the original. Judging by it contents, the *Account* was composed from Russian and Greek sources. We will have to wait for the publication of the complete Greek list to fully appreciate this source.]

1. The holy Apostle and Evangelist St. Luke, a native of Antioch in Syria, practiced two arts: the art of healing

human ills and the art of painting icons, which he followed all his life. He was later numbered among the apostles of Christ God. And he wrote one of the Gospels and preached the Good News to the entire world. He painted the image of the likeness of the most holy Queen of Heaven, the Mother of God, during her lifetime, and showed it to her to see if it pleased her. She turned her eyes to him and said with great joy, "May my grace be with you always!" and then she repeated the prophecy that had been spoken previously: "For from henceforth, all generations shall call me blessed." Afterwards, St. Luke painted other images of the most Holy Mother of God.

2. The holy Apostle Ananias was the slave of Abgar, the king of Edessa, and was sent by him with a letter to Jesus Christ to request him to come and heal the king of his leprosy, or to make his godly likeness, for Ananias was a skilled artist. At that time, Jesus Christ walked in the flesh in Galilee, teaching the people. And there Ananias saw Christ, and going to a secret place, painted Christ's image.

3. The holy and righteous Nicodemus, formerly a prince of the Jews, believed in Christ and was secretly his disciple. When later Nicodemus saw him crucified and beheld the fearful signs accompanying that event, he was allowed to render Christ the service of taking his body from the cross and burying it, with the help of Joseph of Arimathea and John the Divine. After the Crucifixion, this Nicodemus painted the image of the Savior in the city of Birit for the veneration of the Christians, since from his childhood he had been skilled in painting images. You may read about this in the *Prologue* for the month of October.

4. St. Martin, bishop of Balkuria, a disciple of St. Peter, painted many images, including an image of the most holy Mother of God in a church which he founded. And when this church was burnt, people saw angels carry that

holy image out of the fire. Later he painted the image of the holy apostles Ss. Peter and Paul with which St. Sylvester, the pope of Rome, healed St. Constantine the emperor, and many other icons.

5. The faithful Emperor Manuel the Greek painted many holy icons with his own hand out of the love which he had for Christ. He painted the image of the Savior—called the Savior with the Golden Robe—seated on a throne holding the Gospel and blessing with his right hand, placed it in his residence, and prayed before it with faith. In this icon, the right hand of the Savior appears not to bless but to point with one finger. [**SAKHAROV**: We possesses a separate account of the Emperor Manual's vision of the Savior's image. It has been edited by J. M. Sneguireff, in an annex of his book *Monuments of Muscovite Antiquity.*]

6. St. Lazarus, bishop of Evandria, was a Constantinopolitan icon-painter who painted many holy icons. He painted the image of St. John the Forerunner which was wonderful to behold and for which he was persecuted by the iconoclastic emperor who ordered that both his hands be cut off and that he be thrown into prison. St. Lazarus was released in the days of the Empress Theodora, and when he died in the Lord, he was buried in the Evandria Monastery.

7. St. Germanus was the patriarch of Constantinople whom the writings describe as an icon-painter. This Germanus painted the image of the most holy Mother of God on the pillar, which is in Lydda. This holy icon worked miracles during the time of the iconoclastic heresy. See the account in the *Sbornik* which tells how Germanus sent this icon by sea with a letter to Pope Gregory of Rome.

8. The venerable Palestinian Father, St. Jerome the icon-painter is written about in the book *The New Heaven*, which tells how he painted a truly wonderful

icon of the most holy Mother of God.

9. Our venerable Fathers the Greek iconographers who were summoned by the Most Holy Mother of God herself and were sent to Russia to paint in the Kievan Monastery of the Caves. See the account in the *Paterikon of the Monastery of the Caves*. The incorrupt remains of these iconographers are venerated in the Kievan caves.

10. St. Methodius, bishop of Moravia, painted many icons when he lived in Thessalonica, and when he went with his brother Cyril to the Serbians, Slavonic Bulgarians, and Russians, he baptized the pagans in the name of the Father and of the Son and of the Holy Spirit and preached the Gospel of Christ to them. He came to the land of Russia where he painted the image of the Second Coming of Christ on a panel, showing Christ giving the Kingdom of God to the righteous and various punishments to sinners. And when the Grand Duke Vladimir of Kiev was searching for the true faith (for he was as yet unbaptized), Ss. Methodius and Cyril showed him the painted image of Christ. And then the prince and all the people believed in Christ and all the Slavs, Russians, and Bulgarians were baptized once they had seen the paradise given to the saints and the torture and burning fire given to the faithless. And so they came to be Christians by beholding a painted icon.

11. Our venerable Father St. Alipy, the wonderworker of the Caves Monastery was a Kievan iconographer. This St. Alipy painted many marvelous icons, and his incorrupt remains are venerated in the Kievan Caves to this day. See the account of him in the book *The Paterikon of the Caves Monastery*.

12. The venerable Father St. Gregory, wonderworker of the Caves Monastery, was a Kievan icon-painter. This St. Gregory painted many wonder-working icons which are found here in the land of Russia. He worked with St. Alipy, and his incorrupt remains are venerated in the Kiev Caves.

13. St. Peter, metropolitan of Moscow and all Russia, a wonderworker, painted many holy icons. When he was abbot of the monastery of the Savior on the Rata River, he painted an image of the most holy Mother of God and gave it to Maximus, metropolitan of all Russia. After the death of this Maximus, Peter himself became metropolitan and painted other icons. See the account of him in his *Life*.

14. St. Theodore, archbishop of Rostov, the relative of St. Sergius, painted holy icons. When he was the abbot of the Simonov Monastery in Moscow, he painted a wonderful image of his uncle, St. Sergius the Wonderworker. And in Moscow there can be found icons of the *Deisis* which he painted in the Church of St. Nicholas on the Bolvanovka.

15. St. Andrei, icon painter of Radonezh, surnamed Rublev, who painted many wonderful and beautiful holy icons. This Andrei at first lived under obedience to the venerable Father Nikon of Radonezh who ordered him to paint the icon of the Holy Trinity for that monastery in honor of his spiritual father, St. Sergius the Wonderworker. Afterwards he lived in the Andronikov Monastery with his friend Daniel, and there he died.

16. The venerable Father Daniel, called *the Black*, was the friend and fellow-ascetic of Father Andrei, and painted many holy icons. This Daniel lived inseparably with Andrei, and after Andrei's death, Daniel went to join him. In the Monastery of the Holy Savior of the venerable Fathers Andronik and Sava, he painted the wall paintings and the portable icons for the monastery church at the order of hegumen Alexander. There he was granted the favor to fall asleep in the Lord. See the account of him in the *Life* of St. Nikon.

17. The venerable St. Ananias, a priest in the Monastery of St. Anthony the Roman the Wonderworker of Novgorod, painted wonderful icons of many holy wonderworkers. See the account of him in the *Life* of St. Anthony the Roman.

18. The venerable Father St. Ignatius, called the Golden, a wonderful icon-painter who lived in the Simonov Monastery and was a fellow-ascetic of the venerable St. Cyril of Belozersk. He painted many holy icons. See the account of him in the *Life* of St. Jonah.

19. The venerable Father Dionysius the Wonder-worker of Glushitsa and Vologda, painted many holy icons which can be found in Russia to this day. See the account in his *Life*.

20. The wonderful and marvelous Macarius, metropolitan of Moscow and all Russia, painted many holy icons and wrote the lives of the holy fathers. This was the Metropolitan Macarius who painted the image of the Dormition of the Most Holy Mother of God and at the council laid down the regulation about the painting of icons.

21. The holy bishop, St. Athanasius, metropolitan of Moscow and all Russia, painted many holy icons.

22. The venerable Father St. Anthony the Wonder-worker, hegumen of Siya, painted many holy icons. This St. Anthony painted the image of the Holy Trinity in his monastery. See the account of him in his *Life*.

23. The venerable St. Adrian, hegumen of Poshekhonsk, painted many holy icons. This St. Adrian at first lived in the Korneliev Monastery, and later in his own hermitage, where he was murdered by robbers.

24. The pure Father St. Gennadius, who lived in the Monastery of St. Elijah in Chernigov, painted a wonder-working icon of the most holy Mother of God. See the account of him in the book *The Wet Fleece*. [SAKHAROV: This Father Gennadius in the world was named Grigorii Konstantinovitch Dubinskii and lived in the year 1658.]

English translation by Thomas Drain.

B) The Account of Holy Iconographers [2]

[BUSLAEV: In conclusion …, we should draw attention to *The Account of Holy Iconographers* which is part of the manuscript of Count Stroganov (without miniatures). Among the foreign iconographers mentioned, we find the following: the Evangelist Luke, the Apostle Ananias, St. Nicodemus, Bishop Martin the disciple of St. Peter, Bishop Methodius of Moravia, Emperor Manuel Paleologue, Bishop Lazarus of Evandria, Patriarch Germanus of Constantinople, the venerable Jerome of Palestine (with a reference to *The New Heaven*).[3]

As for Russian iconographers or those who worked in Russia, I here present the exact text.]

1. Metropolitan Peter: St. Peter, metropolitan of Moscow and all Russia, painted numerous holy icons when he was hegumen of the Monastery of the Savior. He himself painted the icon of the most holy Mother of God and presented it as a gift to St. Maximus, metropolitan of all Russia. When Metropolitan Maximus died, the Mother of God herself, speaking from the icon, blessed Peter to become the next metropolitan, and he did succeed Maximus as metropolitan. You can read about the icon in his *Life* [BUSLAEV: or even here, that is, in the article on the icons of the Mother of God.]

2. Metropolitan Macarius: The holy, very admirable, and miraculous Macarius, metropolitan of Moscow and wonderworker of all Russia, painted numerous holy icons and wrote books and the lives of the holy Fathers for the whole year, in the order of their celebration, as no one else among the saints of Russia had ever done. He also ordered that the Russian saints be celebrated and set out this rule during the council. He painted this image of the Dormition of the most holy Mother of God.

3. Metropolitan Athanasius: The most holy and venerable Athanasius, metropolitan of Moscow and all Rus-

sia, painted numerous holy and miraculous icons.

4. Archbishop Theodore: Archbishop St. Theodore the Wonderworker of Rostov, nephew of St. Sergius, painted numerous holy icons in the Monastery of St. Simon in Moscow. He painted an icon of his uncle, Sergius, the venerable wonderworker. Here in Moscow, there are icons painted by him and a Deisis in St. Nicholas' church, on Bolvanovka Street.

5. Alipy the Iconographer: The venerable monk priest, Father Alipy, wonderworker of the Monastery of the Caves and iconographer of Kiev, painted numerous miraculous icons. The angels of the Lord helped him and painted icons as though they were his disciples, asking him if what they had painted pleased him. He lies even to this day, uncorrupted, in the Caves of Kiev where he performs miracles.

6. Gregory the Iconographer: The venerable Father Gregory of the Caves, iconographer of Kiev, painted numerous holy and miraculous icons that are found here in Russia. He and the venerable Alipy were companions in fasting. He lies uncorrupted in the Caves.

7. Dionysius of Glushitsa: The venerable Father Dionysius, hegumen of Glushitsa and wonderworker of Vologda, painted numerous holy icons. His miraculous icons are found here in Russia. He accomplished many miracles around his tomb in the Monastery of the Intercession.

8. Anthony the Wonderworker: The venerable Father Anthony, hegumen of Siya and wonderworker of Kolmogori, who lived near the Arctic Ocean, painted numerous holy icons as well as the image of the most holy Trinity in his monastery. One time the church caught fire, but the icon came out by itself undamaged, settling down like a dove in the hands of the venerable Alipy. See Alipy's *Life*.

9. Adrian the Hegumen: The venerable martyr

Adrian, hegumen of Poshekhonsk and wonderworker of Vologda, painted numerous holy icons. He lived first in Cornelius' monastery and then in his own hermitage where he was killed by brigands. His monastery, named for the Dormition, is now found near the village of Byely.

10. Andrei Rublev the Iconographer: The venerable Father Andrei of Radonezh, iconographer, surnamed Rublev, painted numerous holy icons, all miraculous. It is said of him, in the Stoglav Council [the Council of One Hundred Chapters, Moscow, 1551] by wonderworking Metropolitan St. Macarius that icons must be painted using Andrei as a model, and that iconographers should not follow their own judgments. He had previously lived as a disciple of the venerable Father Nikon of Radonezh who ordered an icon of the most holy Trinity to be painted in his presence to honor his spiritual father, the wonderworking St. Sergius.

11. Daniel the Iconographer: The venerable Father Daniel, a companion in fasting of Andrei Rublev, was a well-known iconographer surnamed the Black. He painted numerous holy icons with Andrei Rublev. He was everywhere Andrei's inseparable friend. As death approached, he and Andrei came to Moscow to the Monastery of the Savior where they had both been summoned by the hegumen Alexander, a disciple of St. Andronik. Along with the venerable Fathers Andronik and Saba, they covered the church with frescoes and icons and there received the grace of falling asleep in the Lord, as it is written about them in the *Life* of St. Nikon.

12. Ignatius Zlaty the Iconographer: The venerable Father Ignatius Zlaty [the Golden], iconographer of the Monastery of St. Simeon, was a companion in fasting of the venerable Cyril of Belozersk. He painted numerous holy and miraculous icons. See the *Life* of Metropolitan St. Jonas who spoke often with him.

13. Ananias the Wonderworker: The venerable Fa-

ther Ananias, priest, was a marvelous iconographer in the Monastery of St. Anthony the Roman, wonderworker of Novgorod. He painted numerous holy and miraculous icons. See the *Life* of the venerable Anthony the Roman.

14. The Greek Painters: The venerable Fathers, a group of Greek iconographers, were commissioned and sent to Russia by the most holy Mother of God herself to paint the Monastery of the Kievan Caves. She also miraculously gave them an advance on their salary. On this subject, see the book of the Pechersky Fathers. They lie uncorrupted, 12 of them, in the Caves.

15. Gennadius the Monk: The venerable Father Gennadius of Chernigov lived in the Monastery of St. Elijah and painted a miraculous icon of the most holy Mother of God which cried for a long time in 1760. See the book *The Wet Fleece*.

Commentaries on the Two Accounts [Bigham]

1. The two *Accounts* are very similar, but not identical; the saints are not even in the same order, nor arranged in chronological sequence, even though the same names appear in both lists. The source on which they are based, the manuscript of the Stroganov podlinnik—a sketchbook filled with icon designs—published at the end of the 16th century has apparently been lost. See *An Iconographer's Patternbook: The Stroganov Tradition* (Christopher Kelley, tr., Torrance, California, Oakwood Publications, 1992, p. ix). We are therefore unable to compare the two lists with the original.

2. Ananias the Apostle: The story of King Abgar is well-known as is the role of Ananias the ambassador artist, but it seems that the *Accounts* are the first documents in which Ananias is numbered among the saints.

3. Nicodemus the Righteous: We have found no other reference naming Nicodemus as an iconographer.

4. Bishop Marmun or Martin: The two names desig-

nate the same person, but he and any historical source are unknown, at least to the author.

5. Manuel the King: The reference is to Manuel II Paleologue (1391-1425). According to the *Oxford Dictionary of Byzantium* (vol. 2, Oxford University Press, pp. 1291-1292), Manuel wrote many theological treatises and finished his life in a monastery, having taken the name of Matthew. We have, however, found nothing to confirm that Manuel was an iconographer or considered to be a saint.

6. Germanus the Patriarch: Even though Patriarch Germanus was a witness for the orthodoxy of icons at the beginning of Byzantine iconoclasm, he is not recognized as an iconographer in the sources we have consulted.

7. Jerome of Palestine: Our sources know nothing of St. Jerome the iconographer of Palestine.

8. In the sources we have consulted, we have not been able to confirm that Ignatius Zlaty the Iconographer, Metropolitan Athanasius, Anthony the Wonderworker, and Gennadius the Monk have a place among the saint iconographers. Further research, however, may show that they in deed do belong to this category of saints.

NOTES for the two Russian Documents

1. The translation is based on the Russian text found in I. P. Sakharov, "Skazanie o ikonopistzakh," *Issledovania o russkom ikonopissanii,* St. Petersburg, 1849, vol. 2, Annex V, pp. 12-14.

2. The translation is based on the Russian text found in F. Buslaev, *Istoricherskie Ochersi Rousskoi Narodnoi Clovesnocti i Iskusstva* [Historical Sketch of Russian Folklore], vol. II, St.-Petersburg, 1861, pp. 378-380.

3. Buslaev's explanatory note #3: "One of the two podlinniki [collections of sketches used by iconographers] of Count S. G. Stroganov contains a curious *Account of the Holy Iconographers.* Among the Russian iconographers mentioned are the following: Metropolitans Peter, Mac-

arius, Athanasius; Archbishop Theodore of Rostov; Alipy and Gregory of the Caves; Dionysius of Glushitsa; Anthony of Siya; Adrian of Posherkonsk and Vologda; Andrei of Radonezh, surnamed Rublev, and Daniel the Black; Ignatius Zlaty [the Golden] iconographer of the Monastery of St. Simeon; Ananias of the Monastery of Anthony the Roman; and Gennadius of Chernigov. Beside each iconographer's name, both foreign and Russian, we find a short note on the characteristics of their works ... with references to *The Chronographer*, *The New Heaven* by Galiatovsky, *The Wet Fleece* by Dimitri of Rostov etc. Beside the name of Manuel Paleologue, there is the well-known story of the Savior's image that went from St. Vladimir to Novgorod and Yaroslav and then to Moscow. It is also told how Methodius the Moravian, brother of Constantine the Philosopher [St. Cyril], showed our prince Vladimir the Last Judgment which Methodius had painted himself on a canvas. In so doing, St. Methodius converted Vladimir to Christianity." Buslaev, *Historical Sketch of Russian Folklore*, note 3, pp. 56-57.